Self,
Divided

Also by John Medeiros

Queer Voices: Poetry, Prose, and Pride, co-editor

couplets for a shrinking world

Self, Divided

John Medeiros

HOWLING
BIRD
PRESS

Nonfiction Prize Winner

Howling Bird Press
Augsburg University
2211 Riverside Avenue
Minneapolis, MN 55454
612-330-1125

http://engage.augsburg.edu/howlingbird/

Published 2021 by Howling Bird Press
Printed in the United States of America
Book and cover design by Sarah Miner
The text of this book is set in Marion.

Author's Note: This is a work of creative nonfiction largely reflective of the author's memory; some of the specifics have been changed to observe confidentiality.

First Edition

21 22 23 24 25 5 4 3 2 1

This book is printed on acid-free paper.

For my brother, Bobby,
without whom I could never be.

Although Gemini is a light, airy sign, its symbol—the twins—represents duality: dark and light, good and bad, day and night, heaven and earth. There are many stories that draw on this theme of opposites. Your life journey is concerned with learning to work with your twin nature.

—*Gemini Horoscope*

It is necessary to assert the insignificance of individuality to make mortality bearable.

—Mark Doty, *Dog Years*

Prologue

As any identical twin will tell you, we are two halves of a larger whole. Yet while our language is not always singular (as the previous sentence itself illustrates), we live with the yearning to set ourselves apart. My twin brother and I have learned what it is like to share a special intuitive connection that is stronger than that between other siblings. We have both struggled with being treated as oddities simply because of our twinship, and we have had to learn how to assert our independence.

As a gay man living with Human Immunodeficiency Virus (HIV) disease whose identical twin brother is both heterosexual and HIV-negative, I have written this memoir to address themes of identity, family, and mortality. Throughout my life, I participated in numerous clinical trials and I have taken scores of medical treatments, including fish oil chocolate bars, aerosolized pentamidine, Zidovudine (AZT), Videx (ddI), Zerit (d4T), Epivir (3TC), and Interleukin-2 (IL-2), to name just a few.

In the early 1990s, my brother and I took part in an experimental gene therapy study with the National Institutes of Health in Bethesda, Maryland. Far more than what I learned medically, I came to understand my identity as a twin, to appreciate my connection with my brother, and to have a richer sense of self. *Self, Divided* represents the struggle to find an identity separate from my brother—an identity that includes my own homosexuality and subsequent addition of HIV into my personal genetic makeup. And only after I fully embraced those pieces of my identity that distinguish me from my twin, did I take part in the study—a procedure that has forever melded us.

I marvel at how far medical science has come, even as I recognize how much farther it needs to go. It is, admittedly, very challenging to go back to a time when I was faced with an undefeatable virus, writing today during the COVID-19 pandemic, when the entire world is now faced once again with a seemingly undefeatable virus. It's hard to shake the feeling that no one should have to face this more than once in a lifetime.

In the pages that follow, there are moments where the narrative is inseparable from my twin's. At these times the text spans the entire page. And there are times when the narrative contains moments of oneness and individuality. At these times the text appears in a narrower column.

Self, Divided is a reflection on what it means to experience life not as a solitary observer, but as a constant part of someone else's identity. This is a story about the quest for individuality in a world where we are always connected, in one way or another, to others around us.

1.

Evening in Tacoma Park, Maryland, anxiously awaiting the start of day. After almost two years, my brother Bobby and I had been called to the National Institutes of Health to be considered for a gene therapy study for identical twins—one HIV-positive, the other HIV-negative. Was it coincidence or divine intervention that on the eve of meeting the beast face to face, we had watched a television movie about two twins, Bob, and his HIV-positive brother, Tom, enrolled in a bone marrow study at Johns Hopkins University?

Perhaps if my brother and I had been more in tune with our shared nature as children, we could have forecast the outcome of our adult lives. Or perhaps we knew all along that as identical twins, we each needed the other to survive. As I sat on that research campus, I kept thinking, *here I am, twenty-nine years old, awaiting treatment to prolong my life.* A doctor had once told me: *You'll never make it to thirty.* (He later moved it up to thirty-five.) Still, at twenty-nine, I was not supposed to be strategizing over how to best stay alive. I should have been a different person in a different place. Perhaps a teacher, perhaps a lawyer, anything other than a guinea pig hundreds of miles from home reflecting, too soon in life, on my story.

As with most identical twins, the first person singular does not exist because our stories are inseparable. The closest to *my* is *our*.

Our story begins with us living in an overcrowded apartment: Mom and Dad, our two older sisters, my brother Bobby, and I—six total. At an early age I became aware of the symmetry in our family, though I did not know that *symmetry* was the word for it at the time. Dad, and two boys. Mom, and two girls. There is a sense of balance when looking at us from this perspective.

3

Then there is the realization I have of the number two. Bobby and I; we were two. He was born two minutes before I was.

Two years before that, our sister Debbie was born.

Two years before that, our sister Donna was born.

Two minutes. Two years. Two years. Two girls. Two boys. Two twins. I grew to like math.

It began there, on a clear summer morning in mid-May, in utero. As with all twins, it's ironic to say that we were born at the same time, when for nine months before our birth we occupied the same space. The womb, an egg divided. One fertilized egg finding the need to split itself in half, perhaps to rebel against itself, perhaps to stand alone from any other. Perhaps it was his wish, so my brother tore the egg in half the way a knife tears at flesh. After all, he was the more aggressive. Or perhaps it was my wish because I feared what life would be like facing it alone without him, knowing even then that I needed him.

Regardless, there we were, identical twins in the making, split in half from the very beginning of our conception. Even in the womb our bodies took shape and grew in silent competition. My hand pushing on his belly. His foot kicking my arm. We were crowded in that mutual space with me closer to our mother's heartbeat, him closer to the birth canal. Even then there was no escaping each other.

We became as real to each other as the fluid that nurtured us.

Today I think of what it was like for us in our shared space, squeezed together in that dark universe, feeling that once we were born, we would be rid of the other forever.

We don't remember the story, but we remember what we were told. Perhaps it was nothing like this at all, but because we remember it the same way, it remains that way forever. This much is fact: the pictures were taken when we were infants. And like us, they are identical. Closed eyes, knit hats on our heads, and each of our tiny bodies wrapped in blankets with elephants playing drums and trumpets, as if elephants had such talents. But the one feature different in each of the photographs can be seen on our left feet. One of us (we don't know which) has a toe with fingernail polish on it.

Such a minor detail, undetectable to most. But this detail would somehow define us for years to come and haunt us for the rest of our lives.

It was just fingernail polish, associated with little girls whose parents wanted them to grow up too fast. Fingernail polish: a convenience for others to help tell us apart. We don't know what color it was because the photograph is black and white, but it was certainly closer to black than white, a lighter shade of black. Most likely red.

For years we would argue over this photograph, as if admission to wearing the polish were akin to confessing far greater taboos. And our parents will always keep the secret of who was forced to wear the polish, though it no longer matters.

All that matters now is that it once mattered.

And while we shall never know whose toenail was painted, we will remember this: the tenement where we grew up was in the middle of the block on Peace Street, a street which held a certain power in its name, a name that was both appropriate, with a Catholic hospital standing on the corner, and ironic, because the neighborhood, like our house, was anything but peaceful. In our not-so-tranquil home with sirens passing by regularly, we had the largest room in the house, and everyone, even the guests who rarely visited, had to walk through it to get to any other room. With our parents in one bedroom and the girls in the other, this large, transformed dining room became ours.

As infants together in the same crib we were oblivious to the boundaries between us. It was impossible to tell where one of us ended and where the other began, and we welcomed the fusion and confusion gracefully, peacefully sucking each other's thumb.

Back then we made sounds to imitate in our private world the loud universe around us. Some say it's a private code while scientists call it *cryptophasia*, a secret language used only by twins to communicate with each other. One night in December 1965, when we were all of six months old, we knew exactly what to do when our parents tried to quiet us by separating our cribs and putting them on opposite sides of the room.

Lights out.

Mild clatter.

Little did they know that early the next morning, after a night of restless sleep, they would find both our cribs together in the center of the room as though we had never been separated at all.

2.

Why are twins often viewed as a duality always in conflict? The good twin and the evil twin. A human soul and a dangerous spirit—as if the two are mutually exclusive.

When my brother and I were somewhere between three and four years old, we played tricks with *National Geographic* magazines as a call for attention, a need to establish our place in the larger, natural order of things. Doors were fun to slam. Like most children, we did so with a noise that drew attention. Magazines, with all their wonder and pictures, distracted our parents, and took their attention away. We were intrigued by the power of these two forces, the way they could elicit reactions simply by their existence. In the battle between calling for attention and having it taken away, the calling always won. So it is no wonder that we took the magazines, as many as we could find, and jammed them between the door and its frame, and slammed the door so hard that it was literally pulled from its hinges.

I took delight in this simple destructive behavior. Sharing laughs with my brother was much different than sharing laughs with either of our sisters, because with Bobby, his laughter was more like an extension of mine. The self completing the self. His inhale to my exhale. A fully mutual presence. That's what laughter was, and we welcomed it fully, knowing it was worth any punishment we would later receive. And after all, that was all we wanted.

It seems like just yesterday we were simply boys outrunning each other. Summer wiffleball games in the parking lot and we, tired players, carried our music on our shoulders like heroes—laughing, singing, name-calling. Sticks and stones and such and such.

But I have somehow erased my adolescence, blinked

my way from thirteen to twenty. From hiding deep within the bowels of the closet, feeling something like an ice skate piercing my skull and leaving me bleeding in silent lobotomy, dripping among Barbie Doll cases and has-been Easter dresses, to watching others around me finish law school while I counted T-cells as if they were glass marbles clumsily spilled across the kitchen floor, my hands too blunted to pick them up.

But maybe such thoughts aren't out of the ordinary. Perhaps it's endemic in our family to bypass adolescence and mature faster than our peers. After all, my brother and I are the same age and he has already been married and separated. Similarly, I've had two loves gone awry. What does that say about us?

I once read that with twins, the choice of different friends and partners reflects genetically-based individual tastes and preferences that stem less from their interest in people than it does their desire to be unique.

Has this been our fate all along?

3.

Home. The word surrounds my lips like a breeze struggling to escape the wind: home. There are layers and layers of meaning in these four simple letters. And layers and layers of pain. The Portuguese word (from our father's side of the family) is *saudade*; the English word (from our mother's side), something between nostalgia and longing.

The difference between the two is the pilgrim who never finds his way back.

Our apartment was a tenement bordering the south side of Providence. It was small and crowded, but our parents made it home. There was no dining room, just a larger extension of the living room that converted into a bedroom for Bobby and me when night came. Mom took pride in her decision to purchase sofas that magically transformed them-selves into beds with the pull of a lever and a jerk of a bar. Bobby and I liked them, too, because our beds were like secrets hidden in the bellies of the sofas. It was as though they, too, had secret identities.

Our sisters had their own room. We envied them because it had doors they could open and close at any time. Bobby and I just had archways. *What happens once the doors are closed?* I once asked. *Just girl things*, Bobby said.

From the earliest days of our childhood I learned that privacy was something we could not afford, even as early as nursery school. The school was in a small brick building attached to the Roman Catholic church, with a wire fence around it and large silver doors that revealed a stained glass face of Jesus that watched us from head to toe each day as we entered slowly, single file, with heads bowed as if in prayer. I wonder if Bobby was scared each day as we entered the building in the same way I was. Our teacher at the time was a nun by the name of Sister Michael Linda, a tall thin woman who looked like our mother, only instead of hair, she wore a long blue cloth on her head. She reminded me of Miss Clavel, the nun in the *Madeline* books. Miss Clavel, how tall and thin she stood, towering over all the girls in that Catholic boarding school. I suppose Bobby wouldn't remember Miss Clavel because he never read *Madeline*. It was I who used to read those books silently in the corner of the Knight Memorial Library while he and the other boys in our class made papier-mâché globes in the backroom that always smelled of homemade paste.

It was never said, but boys were not supposed to read *Madeline*.

Good afternoon, Sister Michael Linda whispered, towering over me, her own Madeline, as I left the nap room after waking up before the other children. I mumbled something, making my way to the coloring table, where crayons and a stack of blank manila paper awaited me. Without much thought, I drew a picture of an animal and Sister Michael Linda told me to write my name on it. *Now, Bobby, let's see how well you can spell*, she said. *Why don't you write your name next to the pretty cat you drew?*

She pushed the drawing closer to me.

I thought about what Madeline would do in this situation, what clever things she would conjure up at this very moment. Instead I said nothing. I did not tell her that the cat was really a dog, I simply drew pointed ears on it and added whiskers and a long snaky tail that curled at the end like a fancy question mark. But most importantly, I did not tell her that I was really Tommy—the name everyone called me back then—and that my brother was still sleeping in the nap room. Teachers just assume things with identical twins, and it was always easier to play along with the charade.

Let's go, Bobby. Put your name on it, and then we can put the picture of the pretty kitty cat in your cubby. She continued with eyes so eager they refused to blink.

T-O-M-M-Y, I wrote, smiling, knowing it didn't spell Bobby, but not knowing how to spell anything else. I shrugged my shoulders and watched as Miss Clavel stood before me in her blue confusion. She paused a moment, stiffened her arched back, and finally caught on with a frown. *And it's a dog,* I said, *not a cat.*

And even though my brother slept through one of my earliest memories, I could not have had it without him.

If Sister Michael Linda had paid attention, she would have been able to tell us apart by our little secret: we always wore the same clothes, but with one exception. Bobby's outfit was always blue, or, as our parents used to say, *B for Blue, Bobby.* Mine was always *T for Tan, Tommy.* Dressing this way prevented others from confusing our identities. It was something our mother did for them, not for us.

And so it was that year in nursery school, with Sister Michael Linda standing before me like an idol with no worshipers, only children with miniature hands learning for the first time how to pray, that I discovered what the center meant. It involved a simple heart I drew for my mother on Valentine's Day— mothers are the only valentine a gay child knows. Folding the paper in half, I learned the perfect symmetry of the heart, that when a finger paints a curved line and folds its landscape onto itself, the heart is then complete. That the edges of the heart are round. And the sharpest, most painful part is deep within its center.

It is that center and its symmetry I claimed, even with my own name.

It only worked when I used my middle name, starting only with the central letter. So I began with the letter *m,* and then placed a *t* and an *o* to its left, an *m* and a *y* to its right. *tommy.* With its five letters, its balance and symmetry as perfect as identical twins. I centered my life around my name. I could write it both vertically and horizontally, as with a cross. And the middle letter, the center of it all, could give rise to endless possibilities.

t

o

t o m m y

m

y

After school that day I shared with Bobby the story of Sister Michael Linda and how I had pretended to be him. Walking home from the bus stop, we laughed that laughter that completed us both. And I cherished that moment, knowing, for that day, I was his hero, and we owned the joy of discovering that we were different from others.

This is what life is like when you're a twin: you tap your toe on the crib. You tap your toe on the crib three times because you know that when you tap your toe on the crib three times, by the third time he will always tap back. This is what the tapping is like. You wear a shirt of one color and that color begins with the letter that also begins your first name. And when your first name begins with the letter T you know that you will live a life of tans and teals. And while you wear a shirt of one color, tan or teal, he, too, wears the same shirt, but of a different color, perhaps blue, royal blue, navy blue, sky blue, baby blue, perhaps black, perhaps brown, perhaps beige (but perhaps not beige since beige is too close to tan). His name begins with the letter B because he was born first.

You hide a lot. In closets, in another room. Even when you visit guests on Sunday you hide under the staircase covered with wallpaper that bears pictures of trees and flowers. You find the room on the third floor that no one uses anymore, lock yourself in the bathroom until someone notices (people don't always notice) and when someone notices they ask where you have been and you answer solemnly, *alone*, because that is where you went.

You sleep in the same bed as if sleeping in the same bed were the same as sleeping in the undisturbed womb. You listen late at night for the noises that he makes because sometimes the noises that he makes are the noises that you make and you cannot hear yourself when you are sleeping so instead you listen to the noises that he makes so you can listen to yourself when you're asleep.

You are living proof that no one is ever alone. And so is he.

There are those decisions that pass by in the middle of the night without anyone ever taking notice, and then there are those that are so crucial they determine the outcome of our lives from that day forward. We don't always know when such vital decisions cross our path, and often years will pass before we even realize their significance. Such a decision arrived at our doorstep in 1970, when my brother and I turned five years old.

We had just completed nursery school and were planning to attend kindergarten in September, when our principal met with our parents and asked what they felt about separating us for the first time.

Of the two, Tommy is much more attentive to his studies, Sister Michael Linda said to our parents. *I think you may want to consider having him skip kindergarten altogether and go right into first grade. Academically, I think it would be good for him.*

But is he mature enough? Our parents asked. *I mean, they've never been separated at all. Not once all their lives.*

Sister Michael Linda frowned for a moment. *Then again, both the boys would have fewer difficulties settling into the routine of a new school if they were to attend that school in the same grade, especially since they do not know anybody else. In that way, they'd be taking care of each other.*

Yes, our parents repeated. *They are used to that.*

So for me, skipping a grade would never happen because, as our parents would later put it, my brother and I had to *take care of each other.* Deep down, I like to think the real reason we stayed together was knowing that ours was a force that could not be separated, no matter how hard others tried to do so. For better or for worse, my twin brother and I had a bond so tight no one and no school could pull us apart.

4.

As children we walked in giant steps—our stride unmatchable in our private universe. We stopped and threw pebbles by the handful at cars driving by and we feared no one because we were indestructible. We were twins and others were mere mortals and we felt invincible with our pebbles in our hands, laughing at the sound of each *click clack* as stone brushed up against metal.

But these are the musings of innocent children. We believed the world was indeed our oyster only until the sweet *click clack* was interrupted by the sound of brakes screeching, the first car to stop to remind us of our mortality.

Uh-oh, Bobby said. *Let's get out of here!*

He ran off, but I watched in horror as the car pulled off to the side of the road. The door flew open and spat out a huge, burly man wearing a plaid flannel shirt with the sleeves rolled halfway up his forearms. I ran the same path Bobby took, and the man shouted *Stop!* as he ran in our direction. When Bobby and I made it to the house we cried loud enough for our mother to hear, *Help! Someone's chasing us!*

She appeared magically out of nowhere and sent us into the next room, somehow knowing exactly what we did. When our mother confronted the man at the door, his face reddened with anger.

I wonder if Bobby remembers this story at all. As for me, I can still hear the man shouting at our mother as he spat between his sentences. *Your son threw rocks at my car! What are you going to do about it?*

And with a coolness that we've always loved her for, our mother opened the door to the room where Bobby and I were hiding, took us each brusquely by the arm, and escorted us to where the angry man was waiting. With a smirk on her face, she said to the man, *If you can tell me which one it was, I'd be happy to punish him!*

The man looked confused. It was as if he had never seen a set of twins before in his life. He cursed us with words we had never heard before, mumbled a few more and then left, grumbling along the way.

We were both punished, of course, because that's what happened whenever one of us did something wrong. And the punishment needless to say was effective. It is true that on that day we learned to never throw rocks again, but the real lesson was much more profound. Like Sister Michael Linda had done several years before, this man taught us that as twins, Bobby and I had the power to confuse. To elicit shock. To demand and receive attention. But most importantly, we learned that in order to do so, we each needed the other.

Having this power didn't mean that something within me didn't cry for more. Being an identical twin meant being more than one person; it also meant being incomplete at the same time. So somewhere between the matching of our outfits and the faces we confused, a part of me needed separation from my brother.

Bobby must have felt the same way, too.

With more friends than worries, Bobby was the more social and independent of us. And with more worries than friends, I was more reserved, irritated when things did not go my way. I embarrassed him with my awkward social skills, so wouldn't it only follow logic that he would also want separation from me?

But I knew that day of separation would not come for a long, long time, if ever at all, and instead I found myself searching for ways to not be him. Ways to be completely separate from him. I would later find that freedom through words.

Growing up I was forever eager to read. Words became my refuge, my retreat from the congested world around me, and each word had a different sound that took me to a different place. I played with words. I placed letters together and made up new definitions. I did not know the word at the time, but I became obsessed with palindromes, with knowing

how a thing is going to end simply by understanding
how it began.

As a twin, I was a palindrome. I was the same forwards and back-
wards, my double always looking back at me. This is what life is like
when you're a palindrome: 1. there is no sense of you; 2. you have no
name of your own; 3. you hide while others try to find you.

My palindrome: I'm aloof; a fool am I.

I played with words, and I played with so much
more. From words to dolls to Uncle Manny's farm set.

Perhaps if, at six, I had continued to play with the
plastic white and green farm that sat in our godfather's dining room waiting each night for me to claim
it as my own, or perhaps if I had not followed our
Uncle Manny as he called to me in secret, like in a
game of hide-and-seek, one hand on his mouth the
other on his zipper, I would not be living or dying as
I am. There was no clock ticking among the chickens
in the silo. No disease on my farm in the country.

Years later I would come to acknowledge how my
godfather violated me, and I would carry that anger
like a torch. It started when I was sitting in the par-
lor with the cows and the sheep when my godfather
called my name. *Tommy,* he whispered over the sounds
of chatter in the kitchen. When I approached, his
face was charted like lines on a map and stretched
into a smile to offer me a sip from his glass of beer.
Basic as always, his clothes fell on him anonymously,
as if to imply that underneath his shoddy, white
dress shirt and dark beige khakis there could never
be a man of a thousand colors.

His deception was part of his charm.

His eyes focused on me like two black hawks as
I circled the room. They fluttered as they followed
me when I left the kitchen and they resumed their
stare when I returned. This was what I would later

call his sixth sense. His ability to track me down wherever I was. His ability to make me feel his presence, even long after his death.

And then there was the bump on the side of his left hand which made me quiver whenever I saw it. *Just a little something that happened when it got caught in the screen door,* he told me, pushing the glass across the table in my direction, never bending his fingers even once.

I sat and stared only at the bump.

Go on, touch it. It won't bite. His hand waited for my touch.

Instead I watched the bump that jutted from his hand like an extra finger as he tried to cover his grin, laughing as I washed my mouth clean of the beer's acrid taste.

He smiled at me in his kitchen, face crumpled like an old newspaper, eyes always focused on me. *Say goodnight,* my mother ordered from the next room, thinking it would lend the respect he somehow seemed to deserve. And then just at that moment of goodnight, he lifted his glass to me and made a toast.

Why don't you just stay here with us for the night? He graciously offered. *There's plenty of room, and you only live downstairs. If you decide to go home, you don't have far to go.*

I both loved and needed my godfather because he was one of the only people in my world who never, not once, called me by my brother's name. He had the ability to tell us apart no matter what we were wearing, and he was always aware of my need to be recognized as someone separate from Bobby.

Our parents agreed to the sleepover, secure in the disbelief it would be fun.

Many of the details evade me, but I remember the evening in fragments: the plastic beige radio that caught only two AM stations on its best night, its

orange light aglow like a flashlight sandwiched between bed sheets; the stale scent of alcohol and cigarettes clinging to his breath like stitches to a wound;
his finger, bony and wrinkled, offering itself, poking
its way like a cold thermometer. And in the end me,
standing before the bathroom mirror, brushing my
teeth feverishly, rinsing my mouth clean of the foul
taste of evening.

I should have known by the locked bathroom
door. The scent of the porcelain, cold like the tile
around me. The bathtub's clawed feet that gnawed at
my knees. The feeling that I should not enjoy the
touch of his white hair, fine yet coarse like fiber-
glass, as it paid attention to my hips. The way his
voice hesitated the next morning to say, *Very well,*
when our mother asked from the kitchen how I behaved. How his eyes burned like the beer in his
glass for the rest of the night. For the rest of his life.
Or the way he returned me like a prisoner to his
cell, as if nothing had happened, underwear awk-
wardly backward.

For the next few months my godfather would call
and ask if I wanted to come upstairs to play with the
farm. Only he and I knew what he really meant.
Instead of building a fence to keep the horses from
running wild, I would study the orange glow of the
clock radio on his bedside table as it sprayed light on
us like a miniature moon while we discovered other
games in the twilight of his room. Instead of feeding
the pigs that gathered outside their pen, I would dodge
the broken springs of his bed while his mouth, heavy
and moist, closed itself around me as if I were his
first, or perhaps last, meal.

I soon learned to predict when he would call. Like
a farmer who knows when his fields need harvesting,
I sensed his presence even when he was nowhere to be

seen. My clockwork heart would start to race, and then the phone would ring as if by magic.

The images of him would haunt me for years to follow. I would remember his wrinkled face with its dark eyes deeply set and always looking at me. And I would remember him when I with insomnia sat alone at 3:00 a.m., caught in the TV light like a mosquito in a flashlight, watching the owl on the television screen, shaking at the sound of the tapping of the pine tree on the side of the house like the tick-tock of a bomb. I would remember him whenever I turned out the light and ran to my room and jumped in the bed nearly three feet away so the green and scaly arms underneath could not grab me and pull me under.

I believed in them on purpose.

And I would remember him while lying alone in bed, recalling precisely that moment mixed with fear and pain and pleasure. Afraid to even touch myself, as if I were my own Adam.

And I would remember the sadness I felt when he satisfied himself with me for the last time. I was too young to distinguish weeks from months, learning only later the concept of years. His scent lasting only as long as he hugged me one final time and said, *We cannot do this ever again.*

From that day on, whenever I looked at him, his eyes ceased to be his. They dimmed instead of glowed. I wore my shame on my skin like a scar, where it sat heavy as sin. Yet still I was hungry for his touch. Still I yearned for that moment when I would once again be taken from the farm and told the secret I could never repeat.

Go on, touch it. It won't bite.

That moment never came. Just silence.

I would hold on to that silence until the time of his death. Even as a child I knew there was something frighteningly poetic in the sound his body made as it tumbled down the stairs above me, like an old building being destroyed. At first the air crackled, like the hiss of a brush fire. Then, there was a loud thud. Then another.

One. Two. Three. I remember counting as if I planned the whole event.

Four. Five.

Death has five letters, I said to myself. I stood in the middle of the room like a light house waiting for the diagnosis. My oldest sister accused me of not caring enough to cry, and my mother defended me. *He's too young to understand death.*

Foolish woman, I thought, glowing as if the secret within me were a beacon shining from every pore of my body.

At the time, there was no anger in these scenes. No sense of violation or manipulation. Instead, my godfather simply showed me who I was, and told me I was unique, as if he somehow understood my struggle for my own identity.

I welcomed his joke of calling Bobby *Pete* and me *Repeat,* because deep down I sensed that he understood how silly it was to confuse the two of us. When I was with him the outside world no longer mattered, and for that I embraced him. He saw in me a person completely separate from Bobby, and I loved him for that. That is not to say I loved him for the abuse. Instead, I loved him for teaching me that I was different, that something inimitable existed within me and no one else.

Ours may have been a forbidden secret, but never, ever did it seem wrong. At least not at the time.

And then there were the days following his death. After he died he visited my brother and me daily while we delivered newspapers. We saw him on several occasions waiting for us on the corner of Broad

Street and Moore, standing in the same gray overcoat he always wore. At first, I said nothing, convinced he visited me to remind me that even from beyond the grave he was thinking of me. But each day I saw him I grew increasingly frightened, knowing the dead do not show up on street corners.

For several days he stood there and waited for me to look at him. And for several days I did. Then, perhaps because of the need to let go, I watched him out of the corner of my eye. I did not look him directly in the face. I could feel his eyes upon me, and even so, I looked anyway, and when I did he beckoned me to come to him. The image frightened me and instead I ran down the street as fast as I could throwing newspapers wherever they would land. I pictured only the redness of his eyes as I ran from house to house.

Later that day, in the comfort of our beds, Bobby whispered to me, *Tommy, have you noticed that guy who stands on the corner of Moore Street? He looks exactly like Uncle Manny. How come we never saw him before Uncle Manny died? Do you think—*

Don't be stupid, I interrupted, knowing what he was going to say. *He's dead.*

Sharing with Bobby the secret I held was something I was not willing to do, even though sharing was something twins learn to do at an early age. It was easier for me to pretend I did not notice the man on the corner, and easier still to deny ever having seen him.

From that day on the image never appeared again.

I meant it when I said there was no anger in the scenes I shared with my godfather, but that does not mean there was no anger at all. The anger would come years later, when as a freshman in college I found out that I was not the only child he molested (*molest* a term I've only recently begun to use); he found time to abuse my brother as well.

I remember that, Bobby said only after seeing himself in a mirror standing for the first time in boxer shorts, a gift from his wife, the image reminding him of our godfather's scent as he stood, pendulous, before him.

It was then that I learned to hate my godfather for the first time.

It was as though I saw the exact same experience but in an entirely different way. I saw in my brother a different part of me. A part over which I had no control.

Knowing that the man who, my child's mind thought, showed me my individuality had done the same with my twin brother carried with it a further violation, and I hated him for it, for taking advantage of a part of me when that part was still young and vulnerable.

But much worse was knowing that perhaps he really couldn't tell us apart, after all. My godfather did not make me gay, but he did make me feel unique. It may sound oddly selfish in a way, but the fact that I was not the only one of us that he took an interest in erased everything the experience meant to me. I was not as unique as he led me to believe, and it wasn't until years after his death that I found myself angry with the only person in my world who had persuaded me that he knew me—and loved me—as someone unrivaled in every way.

For better or worse, my experience set a precedent for me very early in life to trust others freely and to offer myself without protecting myself. I should have known all along that, as a twin, such love does not come easily.

5.

The lounge was located on Unit 11 of the inpatient hospital, Warren Grant Magnuson Building, National Institute of Allergies and Infectious Diseases, National Institutes of Health. That is what they called the place, though it was really just a room with a billiard table, a bulletin board announcing the latest arts and crafts schedule, and a telephone that received only incoming calls. I came here to meet some other *visitors*, as we were called, but there seemed to be no one else around. And just as I turned to make my way back to my room, I heard a voice whisper ahead of me, *Shoot pool?*

I looked up and there standing before me was a man no larger than a boy. His hair was thin, his face red and too large for a body his size. He was wearing blue pajamas.

Sure, I said, putting down the magazine in my hand. I didn't really want to play pool, but the next thing I knew I was racking the balls and concentrating on making sure that they alternated—one striped, one solid. Only recently had I begun to use the terms *striped* and *solid*.

Growing up, Bobby and I always referred to billiard balls as *high* (everything above the eight ball) and *low* (everything below).

I started at the top of the rack and worked my way down the left side of the triangle, across the bottom, and back up the right side, alternating balls— high, low, striped, solid—spiraling inward until the eight ball landed perfectly, like a bull's-eye, in the center.

Ironic, I thought, to have a low ball at each vertex, as if what keeps the structure together is its weakest points. At that moment such thoughts seemed to make perfect sense.

The game was not terribly exciting. I beat him in less than thirty minutes, and when it was over, I said nothing and instead retrieved the eight ball from the side pocket. *Name's Charlie*, he said. *How long you been here?*

I'm John. I arrived yesterday, but I just checked in today. Charlie was watching me out of the corner of his eye like a child waiting for the punch line of a joke. I said nothing, and to his dissatisfaction, I picked up a nearby magazine and headed to my room.

I expected things to be a bit more hectic, the way they'd be in an episode of *ER*. Instead, the silence hummed. The whiteness of the walls surrounded me like an endless echo. With each moment the room grew smaller and smaller until it became too familiar too quickly. Sounds repeated themselves because they had nothing else to do, and I searched each corner for a story—something, anything to stretch the moments. I exhausted the lounge, and I moved on to new territory.

My hospital room. Somewhere in it there was a story just waiting to get out, like a prisoner who tastes his freedom in the sweat of his sleep. Take the window, for example. To spite the sterility around me, the window had a small hole in it. Maybe it was made by a rock, thrown by a powerful Titan now playing for the Minnesota Twins. Or maybe not, since none of those players are really twins. Not like us. All I knew was that there was a hole in my window and it looked violent, with its shattered glass around the edges and little broken wires that felt around like tired fingers.

I would have done anything for a laugh, so when Charlie popped in, dressed in his own hospital johnny to wish me well, I pointed to the hole in the window and told him it was made before I arrived, so I was choosing not to take it personally.

He did not laugh; neither did I. We each knew why we were there, and we knew that humor had no place in the process.

He excused himself when the doctors entered my room. *They're a grim lot*, I thought as I watched each of them out of the corner of my eye, wondering what they were learning by examining the charts at the foot of the bed.

See you around, Charlie said, but we both knew he wouldn't. He'd be leaving the next morning.

In unison the doctors nodded and shook their heads and pointed to words that had too many syllables for me to remember. And at once, in perfect choreography, they looked at my face, and then my eyes. They were studying me. They were studying Bobby and me. They were studying the baseline me before I changed into something else. These doctors were students and I was part of their lesson plan.

And after studying their subject for a few more minutes, they mumbled amongst themselves in some strange, shared dialect while shaking their heads and pointing at me as though I would not notice, comparing notes along the way. I looked away and examined the flawed window, its broken glass, its quiet pane. It reminded me of our fractured childhood, when everyone thought of my brother and me as one. When all I wanted to do was split myself in half so that part of me could embrace him the way a boy should embrace his brother, and part of me could avoid him and be an only child.

When my brother and I lived our lives together, we lived as one self, divided.

Good luck, I said, waving goodbye to Charlie, knowing he had already left and that it was too late for him to hear me.

Lucky Charlie. He was an only child.

In that starchy hospital bed, I was watching TV and eating soup from a Styrofoam bowl when another study doctor entered the room. He was a short man, I'd guess in his mid-forties, balding on top, his hair graying at the temples. He was carrying a clipboard and a stethoscope hung loosely around his neck. He lifted his eyes from the sheet of paper he was reading and said without asking, *So, how are we doing today* . . . and then paused. He did not know my name, and he sensed that I knew this. He fumbled with the papers on his clipboard, searching for the answer.

He was a rotund and jolly man who chuckled after every other sentence when he spoke. From the view from my bed, he was more round than tall, and his mouth had one of those permanent smiles and opened and closed mechanically like a puppet. I thought to myself that if I were to describe this man exactly as he was, it would seem terribly stereotypical to anyone who listened. But somehow, the stereotype is what he deserves.

It is best for you to rest as much as possible today, so try not to do anything too strenuous. Tomorrow is your big day.

My big day. I remember how it started with an article I read in the *New York Times* several years before. It wasn't uncommon for the media to exploit every scientific idea related to AIDS and expose it like it was a cure. I was aware of that, and therefore skeptical whenever I read anything concerning AIDS therapies.

But this was different. This was a special study at the National Institutes of Health, one designed especially for Bobby and me. It involved identical twins, one HIV-positive, the other HIV-negative. The study would somehow transplant the bone marrow of the HIV-negative twin into the HIV-positive twin.

Simple idea, I thought, but risky. At the time, genes did not strike me as something man should tamper with, especially if that man is the federal government.

The article ended with a phone number to call for additional information. The contact was a woman with a fast, energetic voice, the type one must pay attention to or the conversation becomes lost before it has even begun.

Oh, that study, she said. *We are no longer taking patients for that study. But we are waiting for the FDA to approve other studies involving discordant identical twins. If you'd like, I can put your name on a list and contact you when your name comes up.*

I agreed to be added to the waiting list, and she went on to say that there were a couple hundred names before mine, and not to expect a phone call anytime soon.

Discordant? I said to myself, hanging up the phone. *How can we be discordant if we're identical?*

6.

Bobby and I arrived together at Edmund W. Flynn Elementary School on a clear September day at seven o'clock in the morning, eagerly awaiting first grade. The school bell rang as students scurried about clutching notebooks and pencils. Doors opened and doors closed. Announcements boomed over loudspeakers, and commotions popped up in front of water fountains where boys and girls pushed and shoved each other to quench their thirst before their school day began. This was a place that was new to us, an enchanted forest erected in the middle of a city block, and we approached it with both interest and caution.

Sometime between music class and lunch Miss Matthews announced to the students her plans for a surprise. *We're going to have a party,* she gleefully declared, *with soda and cake. It's going to be a celebration.* I was drawn to her excitement but distrusted her crooked, lipsticked smile.

When we celebrate, we show someone else that we are happy for something they've done. Like when two people get married. Has anyone ever been to a wedding?

A few hands went up but not mine; I had only seen weddings on television.

Well, for those of you who haven't, we're going to watch one today. At that moment she introduced another set of twins to the class, two girls named Tammy and Pammy (*T for Tammy, Teal; P for Pammy, Pink*). Bobby and I looked at each other in horror and disbelief, sensing something was terribly wrong. *At least our names don't rhyme,* he whispered in my direction, rolling his eyes just after managing a wink.

Looking at my brother and me, and then back at Tammy and Pammy, Miss Matthews went on. *The four of you twins would make such cute, adorable couples.* She clapped her hands gleefully like a cheerleader, only older. Much, much older.

What was she thinking? Surely she had seen twins before. We couldn't be that much of an anomaly. Yet on this day she treated us as though two sets of twins were something that could not go unexploited.

The other students made bouquets of paper roses and Miss Matthews donned Tammy and Pammy with matching veils and Bobby and me with corsages made of tissue paper and blue and white ribbon.

I don't want to do this, I said to Bobby, looking for some indication of how we should behave and what we should do. I felt frighteningly lost.

We got married, the four of us. We stood before the class, each of us a frozen victim not only because the teacher made us participate in this silly vaudeville act, but also because of the other three. We rocked ourselves on display and cursed each other under our breath as we mumbled our vows not out of love but of hatred for the other.

I said, *I do.*

I meant, *I will never do this again.*

I was gay even then, and though I could not name it, I knew that whatever it was that was stirring inside me, I would never, ever get married.

7.

Before the day he walked into my life, long before that day when the virus showed up at my door with that look in his eye that said, *Let me in or I will tell the world your secret,* I remember laughing. Just once. It was as a child, when the boy I wanted to be a boy with forever, pushed me down a hill and shouted, *I am King of the Mountain. Begone!* Each attempt to make it to the top of the hill resulted in the same painful and bumpy ride down. But the pleasure in that boy's eyes! The beauty in his hands spoke to me in an unknown language every time they touched me.

His hand said, *Come.*

His voice said, *Go.*

And I enjoyed the dialogue, with all its excitements and confusions.

His hands caused the laughter I kept locked inside to break loose like a free but wounded bird. I laughed because I didn't know what else to do.

And the laughter made my face hurt.

And the laughter made my teeth hurt.

What's it like to be a twin? Curtis Jensen asked me one day at recess. *I bet it's pretty cool to have a brother who is exactly like you.*

We were huddled together on the playground, preparing ourselves for our science experiment. The crickets announced the summer around us as Curtis carefully took a pencil and poked a hole in a piece of paper and held it to the ground. We watched as the sun recreated itself before our eyes. The eclipse came minutes later. Curtis and I cheered loudly as if for the home team, muffling the sounds of the world around us. The eyes of that boy next to me lit up like forest fire.

The sky is trying to tell us something, he said, excited, and I imagined the softness of his curly hair. The scent of it under my nose as he looked for the crescent moon. The blond on his neck like velvet.

We were a perfect, incendiary match.

My brother and I, I finally replied, *we're not "exactly" alike.*

And watching me out of the corner of his eye, Curtis smiled as he responded, *Yes, I already knew that.*

8.

For nine months prior to our exile into the world, we all live in a cosmos of silence. Though none of us remember what, exactly, that cosmos is like, we do know that there are no sounds in that space, save the nurturing *thum-thum* beat of a mother's heart, and, for some, the breath of a sibling there with us. There are no words in that space for things we cannot comprehend, no symbols with meanings attached. These things only complicate matters. Instead we simply live in an unnamed state of being. It's not until we go through that passage of sound—the shrieking of a mother in pain as she follows the doctor's orders to *push, push* into his hands, or our own crying after learning the first lesson that life has to teach us—that we are forced into a new world: a world of speech and symbols, where all that was silent is now spoken, and all that was nameless must now be named.

And that is how we come to the naming of things.

Mother: Roberta Margaret Medeiros (née Campbell), lying on a gurney just after giving birth.

Father: Robert Joseph Medeiros, waiting in another room.

Hospital: Women and Infants.

Physician: Thomas Fogarty, MD, Irish-Catholic, mid-thirties.

She's been in this room before, or at least one like it. Twice, to be exact. First when our sister Donna was born, and then when our sister Debbie was born. There she lies, fatigued and lonely in her white stretched skin, when an unnamed nurse enters the room and says with a smile on her face, *Congratulations. It's a boy.* And then departs as quickly as she arrived.

Enter Thomas Fogarty, MD, several minutes later to announce the same, *Congratulations. It's a boy.*

Yes, the nurse just told me, says the mother Roberta. *She was here just two minutes ago.*

No, says the physician, looking up from her chart. *She told you about the first one. I'm here to tell you about the second.*

This is the story of our naming. My brother, of course, came into this world fully expected. His name chosen before his birth, a plan awaiting his arrival. It was easy for him to be named: *If it's a boy, we'll name him Robert Joseph, Jr.*

Things are always simpler with single births.

But I was an anonymous surprise, arriving in the world before sonograms and pre-birth announcements. How did this happen? Were there no signs to give me away? A second heartbeat, perhaps? Any extra weight? And of course, the question to supersede all others: what on earth would they name me?

It was a question they struggled with for a while in that hospital room, and for that while, I waded peacefully in my own little world of namelessness.

This much they knew: our mother's father was named Robert, and that name had already been taken.

Our father's father was named John, and it was one our mother disliked.

The doctor's name was Thomas, a name our mother favored.

And that is how I was named. There he was, Robert Joseph, Jr., pre-named with clothes and toys already picked out for him. And there I was, Thomas, newly named after the intimate stranger who delivered me.

But there was something askew in this awful naming of things. With both a father and a brother named John, our father would not be able to explain to his family why he and his wife chose the name Thomas for his son. So, to appease his family and pay homage to the doctor, our parents gave me the legal

name of John Thomas, and, that's what it would re-
main. But my family would know me only as Tommy.

Growing up together as twins I could say my brother and I both had
the same name, a mixture of the two: Tommyorbobby. There was something almost regal about it.

Tommyorbobby, pick up the phone.

Tommyorbobby, take out the trash.

The Tommorbobby Twins responded together, knowing it was easier
to reply to whatever name was being called.

But if truth be told, I liked the name Tommy and
preferred it to John. There was a cadence and a symmetry to it that I admired, although it was eerily close
to Bobby. If truth be told, I accepted it because I
knew of no one else with that name.

9.

Sunday morning, lying in my hospital bed thinking about Bobby, I decided to call him to tell him (and me) how it seemed like everything we had lived for up to that moment was somehow starting to make sense. That everything was suddenly going to turn out for the better. At least that is what I wanted to believe.

But when I called I got his answering machine. I left a short message saying, simply, *Hi, it's me. Tommy. I'm fine. Just wanted to let you know that all is going well, and that I'm thinking about you.*

The reality of the situation was that I was scared as hell, and that I found a certain irony in seeking support from the same person from whom I've spent a lifetime learning to live without. The person who taught me that if I am to live a life worth living, I must live it on my own. I was only then learning what it was like to be dependent on someone whose identity was so intertwined with my own, that being dependent on my brother meant being dependent on myself.

Bobby and I did everything together. We slept together, dressed together, ate meals together, watched cartoons together, dozed off in church together, played baseball together, got into trouble together, got punished together, laughed together, went to school together, came home together, and did homework together—never fully aware that we were two parts of one larger whole. As the Sunday morning sun tapped quietly on my window, I lay listening to the greeting on his answering machine.

After receiving my message Bobby called me back later in the afternoon. *It'll be fine, Bro,* he said, hiding his own fears and concerns, and not too well. *It's gonna take a lot more than that for them to break the Medeiros twins. We've gotten through a lot together. This is just one more thing.*

I hung up the phone without having the conversation that I really wanted to have, because everything he said was absolutely right. Everything he said was everything I needed to hear at that point in time. Yet at the same time, everything he said in no way helped prepare me for that moment.

Being in that hospital room meant more than just being in an experimental treatment protocol for HIV. It meant coming to terms with the entire culmination of all that had been troublesome in our lives. It meant coming to terms with all the identities my brother and I had both assumed up to that moment, and it meant coming to terms with what we had always been, with what we were then and what we would forever be from that moment forward.

Growing up as the younger twin is something Bobby will never be able to understand. But there have been times in my life when being the younger of the two has frightened me horribly because the younger twin by design and definition is simply an imitation of the original. To use the words of our godfather, a *repeat* of the original *Pete.* And as that replica, there is the unspoken expectation that the younger twin should never deviate from the norm established by the older twin. It is as though I have no more of a right to do that than the model has to tell the artist how to paint her. It becomes a matter of knowing one's role in the larger scheme of things.

In our case, it means that Bobby is, and always was, the intended design, and I was never meant to be anything but a replica of that design. A carbon copy. A repetition. And any deviation from that design would mean a lifetime of taking risks and a lifetime of unnecessary failure.

I am not original.

I am not my own person, despite the childhood friends who told me they liked me because of who I was while whispering *Yes, he is really a twin, and looks exactly like his brother,* behind my back, the gossip stabbing into me like tiny syringes into diabetic flesh.

I am, in short, a fake. A copy cat. My entire life an act of plagiarism simply by being born. There is no escaping that feeling. It follows me like a shadow; it always has. It clings to me like an extra layer of skin, and I've spent my life at first trying to shed it, layer by layer never able to fully molt. Eventually, I learned to wear it loosely like hand-me-down clothes.

First his. Then mine.

Perhaps that was why I was in the hospital and my brother was out there in the world, living the life we both should have been living as one.

10.

Summer 1974, and Bobby and I attended Mater Spei Day Camp. The name of the camp always seemed like a misnomer to me: *Mater Spei. Mother of Hope.* Never could this be further from the truth.

Mater Spei Day Camp was run by the Catholic Diocese, and every day for the entire summer we followed the same routine. In the mornings we would pack our bags with our bathing suits and sunblock and then wait for the bus to pick us up in front of St. Michael's Church in South Providence. Our mother would give us each fifty cents and remind us to spend our money wisely (which meant we could spend it on anything but candy). We would then board the bus and wave goodbye as we embarked on the drive that lasted for what seemed like hours, even though Chepachet was less than thirty miles away. And on the bus we would all sing in anticipation the Mater Spei theme song.

Mater Spei is the place for me, that's the only place I want to be. When it's summer and school is out, we go swimming and we laugh about. And we never have a worry or a care. Well, if you ask me where there's lots of fun, Mater Spei, Mater Spei that's where, that's where. Mater Spei, Mater Spei that's where.

When the busload of us arrived, we lined up in two straight lines. Change in our pockets, bags on our shoulders. And like good Christian soldiers we said our morning prayers in an open field, with the sunshine our only witness. And only when we finished our morning rituals did we then break up into smaller groups.

At that time my brother and I were still being grouped together, no matter where we were or what we were doing. Separating us was something teachers would later do. We came to accept the reality and learned that keeping us together was always more entertaining. This was especially true at camp, and because camp was supposed to be about having fun, keeping us together was inevitable.

One day during arts and crafts class we sat with our tie-dyed shirts that we made the day before and tried to make sense of the yarn and twigs on the table before us. The arts and crafts counselor was a bright-eyed girl with long brown hair and a name tag that read *Susie*, which hung on the tee shirt that sported a grinning David Cassidy with a caption under this face that read *I Think I Love You.*

Today we are going to make God's-eyes, Susie beamed, as if any of us in the class knew what she was talking about. And at that moment she held up a completed specimen. Apparently a God's-eye consisted of two popsicle sticks held together in the shape of a cross, tied together with pieces of yarn woven into a pattern to create a diamond shape. Different colored yarn then followed to create larger diamonds, as if God's eye was a bull's-eye in the center of a diamond-shaped, rainbow-colored target.

See! She said a bit too enthusiastically. *This is what the final product will look like.* Fully comprehending the process behind the art, Bobby gathered his materials and wisely moved to another bench, blocking out the rest of us, obviously hoping to avoid Susie's interruptive outbursts.

And I started to work on my creation with Susie by my side. She guided me through the process, and as she did so, she went on to tell me that God's-eyes were originally made by the Native people of Mexico.

But why are they called God's-eyes? I asked, a bit puzzled, ultimately weaving my yarn with rapid acuity.

Oh, that's easy, she said, as if being interviewed. *People placed God's-eyes on the altars in church so that God could watch over them and protect them.*

I held my God's-eye in my hand as if it were some magical mirror from a fairy tale, thinking that perhaps it might talk to me and answer my questions. *Is he watching over us now?* I asked.

Oh, yes! Susie said emphatically. At that moment, she put down her model and looked me right in the eye and said, *God is watching you right now. You are unique and wonderful in His eyes, Tommy. And every time you see your God's-eye, you should be reminded that God's eyes are on you!* And then, like a prophet who has done her one good deed, Susie walked away to enlighten some other camper.

I swear she glowed as she did this.

For the first time in my life something new was happening inside me. Not only was I taught that God was watching me, but that He was watching me, and me alone. I was taught that whenever I needed to feel alone, all I needed to do was look inward and see God watching me, and Bobby would be nowhere in sight. And I took comfort in this.

I turned toward the bench where my brother was working and watched as he mastered his artistry, and I asked God at that very moment, *Is it true? Are you really looking at me? Can you really tell me apart from my brother?*

The possibilities of this God's-eye were endless.

I finished my artwork and tied a long piece of yarn around it, and wore it around my neck like a pendant or a precious stone. This was my amulet, my reminder that I was me (and not us), and that God was watching me (and not us) and that even though the world around us (and not me) would see me as a replica of my brother, God would see me as His own, unique creation.

This feeling of freedom burned within, but like most fires it lasted only long enough to do its damage and then petered out. It was then I saw Susie kneeling next to my brother as she held his God's-eye in her hand. I walked closer toward the two of them, and as I did I could faintly make out the words she was saying.

You are unique and wonderful in His eyes, Bobby. And every time you see your God's-eye, you should be reminded that God's eyes are on you!

Like a record repeating itself, Susie got up and moved her way to enlighten—or disillusion—the next innocent camper.

Never was God's eye more blind.

11.

Summer flew by quickly and before we knew it September arrived and Bobby and I were back in school. Like most children, we had now come to accept our school as an institution we were forced to attend whether we wanted to or not. But there was an odd sense of community about it at the same time. Between the teams that gathered together for school-wide scavenger hunts and faces familiar in both the classrooms and on the buses, there were many of us who came to know each other, if for no other reason but for the familiarity of our faces.

But even one year older, Bobby and I could still not deny that others saw spectacle in our twinship. A spectacle to look at. Spectacles as lenses. And like lenses, we came two to a pair.

One morning we were in reading class and our teacher, Miss Faye, entered the room in a slow, vigilant manner. She was a tall, rigid woman in her mid-forties, with short cropped hair slightly graying on the sides. She walked into the classroom like a drill sergeant, back erect, arms by her side, shoulders back, chin pointing out ahead of her, never to the ground below. In later years, when my brother and I would go to Boy Scout meetings to be taught how to walk like a soldier—those meetings I secretly hated, whose oath reminded me to be *morally straight* and whose law required that I be *clean and reverent*, though I had no idea what any of those terms meant—at those meetings when I would try to walk like a soldier Miss Faye's would be the image that would come to mind. Hers was the gait I would mimic.

She approached the classroom with an air of authority, carrying in her right hand a thick red book. She sat at her desk fully aware of the eyes watching her every move. She had a way of commanding attention without ever uttering a word, the way a parent does when you know you've done something wrong. After a few moments, she coughed. Or at least she made a noise that sounded like a cough, and we all watched, slightly surprised that a cough was able to escape the mouth over which Miss Faye had full control. Yet still she coughed, and we watched and studied her next move. A cough, after all, was not in her daily agenda. A cough is not something she planned. And after she coughed, she opened the large bottom drawer of her desk, pulled out a green bottle and slowly poured its contents into one of the small Dixie Cups we saw only when we visited the nurse's office downstairs.

I just need a bit of cough medicine, she said. And then the lesson started. *Class, I would like you to open your books to page 137*, she said, head bowed and watching us over the top rim of her reading glasses. *Page 137.*

I was still opening my book when Bobby raised his hand and said, *Miss Faye, there is no page 137.* He always seemed to get to where we were both going before I did.

Of course there is! She replied, sitting at the desk with her teacher's manual, pointing to it and tapping it with each word. *I'm . . . looking . . . at . . . it . . . right . . . now.*

The other students in the class struggled, all failing to find page 137.

My book only goes up to page 58, Rachel Hunt replied.

Mine, too, said Michael Stevens, the boy in the black sweatshirt who sat with a timer on his desk that went off every thirty minutes so that he could go to the back of the class to play with a set of building blocks because he was, as we were told, hyperactive.

Stop playing games with me, Miss Faye replied, and poured herself another cupful of cough medicine.

At that moment Bobby raised his hand, waited until he was called upon, and, with the most polite tone his voice could muster gently asked, *May I please have a pass to go to the lavatory?* Miss Faye agreed and handed him a pass, and he quietly left the room, leaving the rest of us struggling on page 58.

A few moments passed and Miss Faye asked me to bring my book up to her desk, perhaps thinking we had the wrong books in our hands. She inspected it closely and said, *No, it's the same book. You are all reading the correct book.*

Standing so close to her scared me. Even on the best of days, no matter where she was, it felt like Miss Faye was always towering over me.

It was as though she were standing at attention even when she was sitting down. But today she was especially frightening as she sipped her green cough medicine with its strong and rancid odor.

Miss Faye, I said. *Your teacher's manual is on page 137, but we don't have the teacher's manual. We only have the reading book.*

And looking closely at the instructions contained in the teacher's manual, Miss Faye then ordered, *Class, please turn to page 35. That is the page we should be on.*

I stood there, confused and scared, bearing witness to the fact that this was the first time I had ever seen Miss Faye make a mistake. I knew then something had gone terribly wrong.

Yes? Miss Faye asked. *Is there something else you want? Because if not you may return to your seat.*

May I have a pass to the lavatory, too? I asked. *I really have to go.*

Didn't you just come back? she said. *I'm sure I just gave you pass a minute ago.*

You were going to give me a pass, I lied. *You just haven't done it yet.*

Oh, well then here you are, she replied, handing me a pass, which I grabbed on to with the passion of a prisoner newly released from jail.

I'm not sure why, but I ran downstairs to Principal Angelo's office and when I arrived I was surprised to see Bobby already sitting there, waiting for permission to see him. I sat next to him and asked, *What do you think is going on up there? Isn't Miss Faye acting strange?*

He answered with a wisdom beyond his years. *Can't you tell? She's drunk.*

To this day I'm not sure how he knew this, since all our lives we never knew of anyone who had a drinking problem, and identifying someone with one seemed impossible to do without practice.

At that moment Principal Angelo appeared, and we entered his office with a silence reserved only for church. Bobby did all the talking.

We're here because we're concerned about Miss Faye, he said. *She's acting strange and is really confused. We think she's really sick because she keeps drinking the medicine that she keeps in a bottle hidden in her desk drawer. We just thought you should know.*

He mentioned nothing about her being drunk.

We waited for Principal Angelo to investigate, and when he did, he called our house ten minutes later and asked our mother to come re-trieve us. All we were told was that our teacher was sick and we could go home early. In reality, my brother and I both knew that Principal Angelo was afraid that Bobby would tell the other students what he already knew. And as is the case with all twins, I was implicated by default.

Miss Faye never returned for the rest of the year, and we returned the next day. To the other students, my brother and I were heroes, but between us, it was clear the moment we were in Principal Angelo's office. The lesson would stay with me forever: Bobby was the one who was always one step ahead of me and my fate as his trusty sidekick was sealed forever.

And I remained his sidekick later that year, with a disastrous incident involving the *Guinness Book of World Records*. I was fascinated by the book and the cult following it garnered, and at the same time compelled to buy the latest editions whenever I came across them at garage sales. The book prided itself on documenting world records, but it really featured some of the most astonishing anomalies that the world had ever known. In addition to documenting such fascinating records like the world's worst-selling author, or the world's tallest tree, it also showcased what the rest of the world knew as sideshow freaks. There was the man who was struck by lightning seventeen times. A woman with a thirteen-inch waist. The obligatory eight-foot tall man and, of course, the conjoined twins, Chang and Eng, the original "*Siamese twins.*"

One day that year I brought the most recent edition of the book to school for an oral report. Miss Faye was replaced by a substitute teacher, Miss Davis. Bobby and I affectionately called her Judy because she was our mother's distant cousin. Judy asked each student to bring in a book of their choosing to share with the rest of the class, and where others chose books like the Hardy Boys and Nancy Drew mysteries, I chose the *Guinness Book of World Records* because I was fascinated by so many documented facts and pictures. It was like having an entire set of encyclopedias in one compact volume. Complete with pictures.

And here's a picture of the tallest building, I pointed out. *And here is the world's heaviest man, who was buried in a piano case! And here, the language with the least number of words in it. It's in Africa, where a tribe of people communicate entirely with one sound, which they make by clicking their tongue!* And I taught the other students to click their tongues until we sounded like a classroom of snapped fingers.

I stood fascinated all over again, as if I had just recently discovered the book on my own. And then the moment came when I knew I would risk my own anonymity, not realizing that in doing so, I was putting Bobby's at risk as well.

And here is a picture of the world's first Siamese twins (a term used then which we would later recognize as offensive). I went on to read, *Chang and Eng were born in Siam in 1811 and they were joined at the chest by a narrow band of flesh through which their livers were connected.* I read how they were exhibited in England, and how they even met the Royal Family.

And here it says "They were not allowed to go to France because officials thought that French pregnant women who saw them would also give birth to Siamese twins."

I cleared my throat and read the final passage, *The two men went on to marry two sisters and, together, fathered a total of twenty-one children!*

At that moment, all eyes looked back and forth at my brother and me. I could tell the students were no longer listening to my report. I watched Bobby fidget in his seat, as if I just did something very, very wrong. I did not realize that in the eyes of the other students we were the freaks in the *Guinness Book of World Records.*

Were you guys joined at the chest, too, when you were born? An ignorant Julie Moore asked behind her blond curls, and I couldn't tell if she was being sarcastic or just dimwitted. *'Cuz if you were you could be in this book, too!* She then snapped her gum, even though gum chewing was not permitted. *And maybe your children will be freaks, too!*

There was no stopping the laughter from the rest of the students in the room. My eyes shifted from Miss Davis—who was no longer a distant relative, and instead a teacher waiting for me to somehow explain myself through the laughter—and my brother, as he sat with his head in his hands, hiding his face out of embarrassment.

But I . . . if you look at page . . . Here the only . . .

It was no use. My brother and I were the laughingstock of the classroom with no new insight to offer. I had no choice but to sit down before I completed my oral report.

I sat confused and humiliated. Twins were not a common thing in everyday life. We appeared in books as early as *The Bobbsey Twins*, and in *Heckle and Jeckle* cartoons, and movies like *The Other*, where one twin was evil incarnate and the other a helpless victim of circumstance. But to actually see a live set of twins, where one looks exactly like the other, that was something most children in South Providence did not see on an everyday basis.

That day all I wanted to do was show the other students that though we were unique, twins are also normal people. Like Chang and Eng, my brother and I could change the way others viewed twins, and we could prove that those who were different could also lead normal lives.

But obviously the world didn't want that. Instead, it demanded that we let go of what we considered rational and sensible, and pretend to know things that only freaks know. Like how one felt when the other got slapped. Or what it was like for one of us to read the other's thoughts from at least one classroom away.

Do you feel pain when your brother gets hurt? A student went on to ask.

I sat silent, afraid to tell her that the answer was undoubtedly *yes*.

12.

If anyone could read my thoughts they would know that I never wanted any of this. It's easy for me to say from a hospital bed a thousand miles away, looking back at how our lives turned out. But when we were growing up my brother and I were naive, and that's a dangerous thing for twins to be.

After meeting several of my neighbors, it didn't take me long to realize that *11 East* in that hospital was code for *Beware: Terminally Ill.* I met cancer patients led astray by chemotherapy as they watched their bodies betray them piece by piece from their hospital beds. I saw those whose bodies had grown old faster than the rest of us, and I wondered what their memories were like. How did they grapple with the unpalpable things like telling time? I saw guinea pigs marching to and from their group therapy, and I noticed in each of their faces the same blank expression, in each of their squinting eyes the same unasked question, *Why did this happen to me?*

Perhaps I should have told myself that I was fortunate to have lived the life of a twin because it somehow prepared me to lurk in those 11 East corridors. How else would I have learned what it meant to stand out? How else would I have known how it felt to live my life as a circus freak, cut into pieces like the frogs we dissected in Mrs. Paul's eighth grade biology class, their frail bodies crucified with pins two inches long? The same class where we studied genetics and drew Venn diagrams and learned that, technically, we were *monozygotic* twins, formed when a single fertilized egg splits in two after conception, twins who

46

are genetically alike—same sex, same hair, same eye color, and same blood type? As a twin I learned to live under the scalpel; I took in the scent of formaldehyde and moved comfortably among the ether, because being a twin meant turning heads, invoking curiosity, instilling a desire in others to dissect us and examine us under the microscope and find ways to *figure us out*.

And after all, wasn't that why I was there, in that federally funded research institution on the hill? For others to *figure us out*?

Those were the exact thoughts I wanted to ask my researchers, but they were not the thoughts they wanted to hear. Sometime during the afternoon the nurse came in to check on me and reminded me there was a television if I wanted to watch it.

The remote control is built into the bed, she said, as if this would somehow cause me to reconsider my options, and surprisingly, it did. I found myself watching a program on forensic science and the use of fingerprints and DNA to capture otherwise uncapturable criminals.

Each fingerprint is unique and different, the narrator announced, telling us what we already knew from our earliest science classes. *Each fingerprint distinguishes us one from the other.*

How funny it was to think of fingerprints at that moment, to think of each fingerprint as a unary and discernible feature, even among identical twins.

The comfort I once took as a child was in using a jar of red finger paint and pressing all my fingers onto a sheet of paper and naming my artwork *Me*, as if it were a self-portrait or my own national ID card. But people don't notice fingerprints without the use of a microscope, and the comfort in proving my individuality to them is soon lost on the realities of our daily mirrored existence.

Looking back, perhaps my brother and I could have had a different life together by looking at those things that made us different instead of taking inventory of those things that kept us alike. Take, for example, our scars, each unique only to the body on which it rests, each serving the purpose of a fingerprint by distinguishing us each from the other. Each containing a personal history behind it.

Wearing latex gloves, the nurse carefully and quietly took my vital signs and delivered my medications in a small plastic cup. She finished her routine and left the room, keeping the door slightly ajar, discarding her latex gloves on the way out.

She left behind no fingerprints, I thought to myself, and yet she was most certainly here.

I once read that the nineteenth century medical science of *semiosis*, or *symptomology*, formed the basis of what would later become *semiotics*. The basic tenet was that marks on the human body, such as wounds and scars, should be seen as signs. They conveyed information. The idea of the mark as sign then took on larger, symbolic anthropological value. Every sign mattered. After all, signs become stories and stories become myths and myths create a need for ritual. Doctors and patients both know that scratches heal and sores may disappear, and if they don't, if they linger too long, the body that carries them may not survive.

These were the stories of 11 East. These were the semiotics worth studying if researchers really wanted to learn anything about us.

13.

Instead of candy necklaces that turned our skin into a sticky rainbow of sugar and dye, and instead of sloppily-made God's-eyes that promised nothing more effective than the broken scapular our mother kept by her bedside whenever she felt sick, and instead of school buses that picked us up daily and shipped us away from the city as we gleefully sang the camp's theme song—the next summer would hold a magical promise my brother and I never before experienced. It was the summer of Camp Davis, a camp affiliated with the Boys' and Girls' Clubs. This was a different camp. An overnight camp. A camp with a new song.

Camp Davis was more exciting than I imagined it would be. My brother and I were ten years old, and for the first time in our lives we would be away from our families for two whole weeks. I'm sure Bobby felt the same excitement. The moment the school bus drove down the dirt road and into the giant wooden gates at the edge of the camp, there was an excitement and a fear that was palpable, and perhaps unconsciously I was being made aware, even then, that excitement and fear can never be mutually exclusive, that each feels exactly like the other.

I would be reminded of this years later, walking into a gay bar by myself for the first time, pulse racing with the speed of a hyperactive heart, palms sweating with desire. My body shivering, freezing cold at summer's feverish peak. And I would again be reminded that excitement and fear co-exist in this world, interdependent and interconnected like identical twins, as they did on that day when the virus entered my life through the kisses and words of an unsuspecting lover.

But back then, at the age of ten, at an overnight camp where boys slept only with boys, these lessons were only starting their brew.

Located on one hundred acres on Schoolhouse Pond in Charlestown, Rhode Island, Camp Davis offered a variety of activities. On any given day there was a plethora of opportunities at our fingertips: fishing, sports, theater, swimming, arts and crafts, woodworking, and nature hikes. We lived in small villages with six to eight campers assigned to each of the screened-in cabins. There were two counselors per cabin, and, not surprisingly, Bobby and I were housed together and forced to share the same bunk beds. We had bunk beds at home by this time, so the concept was not new to us, but we still could not deny that there was something very appropriate about twins and bunk beds. Like twins, bunk beds are identical in frame and structure. And like twins, one is not complete without the other; each is destined to always define the other, lest the whole does not exist. Yet even though we had our bunk beds at home in the city, sleeping in those at Camp Davis—my brother always on the top bunk, me always on the bottom—made the experience new and fresh each night. Because there, at the end of the day, when all the other campers went to bed and Bobby lay sound asleep, I was left alone staring out the window next to my bunk.

There, in that lonely camp in the middle of nowhere, the only thing that awaited me was stillness. It was a stillness we were not used to on the city street known as Peace. A stillness that somehow reminded me from where I came. A silence as deafening as a scream.

Silence never sounded so frightening and exciting at the same time.

I think somehow our counselors could see the differences between my brother and me, and they took it upon themselves to promote those differences and make each of us feel unique. Our counselors shared the same cabin with us. My brother's counselor, Rob, was from England, and he took to my brother partly because they shared the same name, and partly because my brother shared his interest in sports.

My counselor, Ian, also from England, was a beautiful brown-haired man who wore shorts with hiking boots and took me on nature walks in the middle of the woods and taught me secrets he taught no one else. I came to relish the sound of the dry and brittle pine needles as they snapped beneath our feet and the scent of the damp summer mornings.

And do you remember what kind this is? Ian asked as we knelt together on the deserted trail, holding in his hand a ghost-shaped leaf.

White oak? I asked with the attention of an A student, eliciting in him that smile and that nod I enjoyed seeing so much.

By summer's end I collected dozens of leaves, assuming the individual characteristics of each one to remind me how very different from my brother I could truly be. On any given day I found myself being spearmint, or red maple, or red sumac, or sassafras—each leaf pulling me like a fine and golden thread through the eye of nature's needle. I had all of this, without my brother ever knowing.

Even when we walked together as part of a larger group, I picked up pine needles as they fell in our path and whispered to Ian as if hypnotized. *A cluster of three needles is red pine, and a cluster of five needles is white pine*, remembering the lesson he taught me: red has three letters, and white has five, one for each needle in the cluster.

Learning about nature was a secret I kept entirely to myself, later telling my brother only that I collected leaves because there was nothing better to do. Feigning boredom seemed the right thing to do because somehow, by de-glamorizing the experience, I could ensure that Bobby would not find any interest in it whatsoever, that this newfound interest was mine and mine alone. Ian showed me a world that existed only for us. A world where I could live without a twin attached to me at all times.

For the rest of the summer I held for Ian a schoolboy crush because he was not only my teacher, he was also my own private hero who taught me that nature was mine for the taking.

14.

Twins reflect one another like little mirrors, and most of the time we don't even notice the reflection until years later, and only in retrospect. Sometimes, entire scenes repeat themselves, as if somehow forgetting the universe in which they first occurred.

Take, for example, sunflowers. I don't remember their smell, or the way their stems felt downy to the touch like a stalk of green velvet. I remember, instead, their height. How they hovered over me like giant periscopes searching the garden's ocean. And how they seemed to follow me with each move I made, inching closer to the sun.

I had never seen flowers like that before. I was always taught that flowers are fragile and delicate things, always drawn by children using subdued yellows and pinks. They are not supposed to be taller than me. They are not supposed to fill me with a dread so maddening that it would force me to cross the street whenever passing the garden in which they grew.

That is, of course, with the exception of Mrs. de Mello's garden, which I walked past each day. Hers was a garden tended with care. Hers was the direct result of years of preparation and travel from an island a thousand miles off the coast of Portugal. And her garden bred sunflowers in beds aplenty. In school I was taught that the sunflower is native to North America and was used by North American Indians for food and pressed to make hair oil. Its seeds produce meal for livestock feed; baked they become a savory treat. How could someone so European master the art of American cultivation?

These were the thoughts that fascinated me while my brother spent summers looking for new ways to impress the girls who lived next door. This summer it was playing football.

They like that, them girls, he would say. Me, I had no interest in them.

Though my brother and I were identical, there were things we had each held on to all our lives because failure to do so meant risking the loss of our individuality. For him, one of those things was sports; for me, it was poetry. So while he played football I secretly scribbled my thoughts.

> *I remember sunflowers the size of wagon wheels*
> *and grape arbors over my head that bore fruit*
> *so plump*
>> *they had the power to intoxicate*
>> *long before contemplating the wine.*
> *Her raspberries, she said, were the fruit of life,*
> *bitter for some,*
> *sweet for others,*
> *and usually both for most.*
> *Her hands were never dirty.*
>
> *Tomatoes grew next to yellow things that, fried,*
>> *made savory sandwiches.*
> *Cucumbers, summer-ripened,*
>> *snapped at the tug.*
>
> *Everything flourished in that garden.*
> *Earthworms were mistaken for little snakes,*
> *while sparrows made their trek from São Miguel*
> *just to see if the rumors were true.*
>
> *The soil was always black,*
> *and her hands were never dirty.*

Only girls write poetry, Bobby said one day after Mrs. Carter commended me on a poem I wrote in fifth grade. *Way to go, Thomasina,* he later said when we got home.

By this time my brother and I only shared physical things: the paper route that consisted of seven streets and over a hundred customers; the hospital at the end of the street; and the house of our friends, Mario and Ricardo de Mello, where we spent so much of our childhood.

15.

In Providence one year later Spring opened her big green hands and showed signs of budding leaves and flowers, and with them thoughts of Ian cropped up in my mind like a sweet summer fragrance. With the speed of a hummingbird, all the lessons he taught me the previous year flashed before my eyes.

Red oak has spiky leaves.

The leaves of the white oak are rounded and shaped like a ghost.

The berries of white sumac are poisonous to the touch.

Red sumac longs to be stroked and to have its berries plucked.

Spearmint, like a jagged teardrop, is wild and grows best when close to the ground.

The sassafras plant has leaves that look like small versions of white oak, and its roots smell like root beer.

Red maple has more sugar in it than any other plant, which explains why its color changes so dramatically in the fall.

Pansies are wild and can be eaten.

It was now summer. Bobby and I were eleven years old, and that meant we would be going, once again, to Camp Davis.

I never mentioned to anyone how I longed to see Ian again.

I remembered asking him at the end of last summer, *Why are your hands so big?*

I stretch them each morning, he said, *so that I can play the piano.*

Piano. Ever since that moment I noticed it in any song that came on the radio. When my mother would watch *The Lawrence Welk Show* on Saturday nights, she would take pleasure in watching Norma Zimmer, the Champagne Lady. But I paid attention to the pianist. Hearing it, I would see Ian, his large hands dancing across the keys while I picked leaves and named them, one by one.

Looking forward to camp this summer? I asked my brother one night when the lights were out, trying to hide the excitement in my voice.

Nah. I don't wanna go this year, Bobby said. *Mom and Dad said I don't have to.*

And as he drifted off to sleep, I welcomed his decision with an open heart. It meant I would be in a world where others (Ian) would not see me as an extension of my brother, a world where others (Ian) would look at me and see only one person, and not two. I would have that universe entirely to myself for a whole week, and there I would happily dwell as my own self.

Serendipity: finding something without losing it. Without really looking for it. This serendipitous moment was handed to me when my eyes were barely open.

I found myself looking forward to summer with the same combination of fear and excitement that I would always associate with camp. I remember waving goodbye as the school bus pulled away from the building, anticipating the moment when I would arrive and my new world would begin.

But this year at Camp Davis this was all that mattered: the cabin had only one counselor, and this one was from America. His name was Scott; he was interested only in the female counselors.

I asked, *Do you know what kind of leaf this is?* He said, *Are you kidding me?*

I wanted to go home.

No one paid attention to me; I was invisible even unto myself. And if anyone asked me I would say that when I walked past mirrors they refused the reflection, that is, until my very last day. The evening before, Scott planned to have all of us campers sleep outdoors without notifying us in advance. It's not that I wasn't prepared (after all, I brought my sleeping bag and a pillow and a flashlight with me), but there was something about the thought of sleeping out-doors that scared me. I asked Scott for permission to stay behind, and when he turned his back and waved his hand in the air, I knew the answer was no. I begged for him to reconsider; I promised to have the cabin clean by morning. I promised to watch over the cabin until the rest of the group returned. I promised anything. And I accidentally called him Ian.

Who the heck is Ian? He asked. *Don't be a sissy, just get your things and get going,* was the only other response Scott gave.

It wasn't just the thought of sleeping outside that scared me. It was also the fact that we were going to hike in the dark to get to the campsite. Under the bright July moon, Scott led us like troops off to war, and we marched, sounding off our *hut-one hut-two's.*

And as we marched Scott somehow pulled ahead of the group, and no matter how we tried to keep his pace, his legs seemed to carry him farther and far-ther away from us, until we stopped marching, and stood lost in the dark wilderness of the moment.

Where did he go? One camper asked.

He was here just a minute ago, another replied.

I said nothing, and instead cried for the loss of it all. The loss of Ian, whom I would never see again.

And I cried for the absence of my brother, who had been, among so many things, my rock and my compass. And I cried for myself and for who I was becoming, and for not understanding what Bobby already seemed to know: that our lives were just beginning to break apart.

I cried for not having my brother with me and felt guilty for wanting it that way.

Suddenly there was a haunting scream that hurled from the dark woods like a banshee at sea, and one of the campers shone his flashlight in the direction from which it came, and there lying on his back was Scott, barely moving under the large branch of a tree strewn across his belly, pinning him down and twisting his right leg in an unnatural contortion. Then, in a matter of seconds, as if his scream were all he could muster, his energy slipped away from him and he passed out before our eyes.

Every single one of us panicked. Three of the campers lifted the branch from his belly, while two of us cleared the way for a comfortable place where we could lie him down.

Oh, man! He's injured! Someone's got to go back and get another counselor, one of the boys said.

Another one said, *Let's just wait here until morning.*

And I, after being silent for a moment, crowded around Scott with the other campers, tears still in my eyes, and asked only one question. *Where's the blood?*

Life slowed down at that moment and we all ran in circles, panicking at the thought of what to do.

Get him to a doctor.

Leave his body alone.

Does anyone know CPR?

Then, in the midst of our crisis, Scott got up on his feet like a new Lazarus and congratulated most of us on our crisis management skills.

That's a game called Lost Pilot, he said. *It's like a fire drill, and we play it sometimes to see how you guys react in emergency situations. And most of you did an excellent job . . . but you,* he said, pointing in my direction, shaking his head and rolling his eyes. *You need to stop crying. And what's with saying there's no blood? You almost gave it away.*

I said nothing for the rest of the night. I did not comment on how there were too many mosquitos hovering at our site. Or that none of us remembered to pack an alarm clock. Or that I missed Ian terribly. Ian, who taught me so much about myself. Who taught me so much about the leaves, including those now gathered at our feet that vaguely resembled poison ivy.

The next morning I found myself waking to the sound of birds calling out to each other. There, standing before me like doctors hovering over an etherized patient, were three other campers, pointing at me and whispering loudly enough for me to hear, *Oh, my God! Do you see that? What do you suppose that is?* I had no idea what they were talking about.

And I did not know how to respond when one of them asked me, *What the heck happened to you?*

Scott rushed over to see what the commotion was about, since all of the campers now gathered around me as if I were on stage.

Holy crap! He shouted when he approached, and then he turned away. *Let's just drop it,* he said, and then ordered us to say nothing else, and to pack our sleeping bags so we could get back to the cabin in time to shower, eat breakfast in the dining hall, and catch the bus back home.

As I walked back to the cabin the other campers kept a noticeable distance before me, as if I were *it* in a game of tag, looking back every now and then, murmuring something only to themselves. It wasn't until we got back to the village when I realized what they were talking about. Because back at the cabin the mirrors decided to make themselves known by showing me my strange and hideous reflection. My face was completely unidentifiable. It was red and swollen to twice its size, and on every centimeter of skin was either a raised bump or something that resembled a pock mark. My eyes were sunken behind the tiny slits of skin that were my eyelids.

I understood then why the others kept their distance; it was because my face was now swollen and round and grotesque beyond recognition, and no one knew why.

I ate breakfast quickly and alone as the other campers turned toward me from time to time, trying to figure out who I was.

I want to go to the infirmary, I told Scott. *I think I need to see the doctor.*

But Scott would have no such thing, and instead told me the bus was leaving in thirty minutes, and I had to be sure to be on it because my family was going to be waiting at the Boys' Club to pick me up. I insisted on seeing the doctor, insisted until I cried. But Scott won the battle, and I ended up getting on the bus, already behind schedule. The other campers, eager to see their families after being away for a week, shouted at me from all directions.

Sitting alone in my seat, my face burned and stung all the way home.

The bus arrived at the Boy's Club twenty minutes behind schedule, and I was relieved to see my father and brother standing outside, waiting for me to take me back home. I couldn't wait for this to be over. I wanted to erase the event as though it had never happened, but I knew my family would want tales of wonder and fascination.

There would be no such thing.

Instead, at the end of that second summer at Camp Davis, I got off the bus and saw Bobby searching for me among the bustling crowd of campers and parents, and I was never happier to see him. I wanted to erase the past week from my mind, to remove the stains that overnight camp seemed to make on my soul. I wanted only to be back once again in the comforts of home, in all its bustling glory.

I saw my brother and I ran to him with arms outstretched, wanting only to embrace the one thing most familiar to me. The moment shattered like untempered glass. As I ran toward Bobby, both he and my father walked right past me, not even recognizing me behind my grotesque facade.

I turned and cried, *Bobby! Dad!* And I watched as they turned and looked at me in disbelief.

Tommy? Bobby asked, hesitating. *Is that you?*

It was me under what would later be diagnosed as a hazardous combination of mosquito bites, sun poisoning, and poison ivy. I was there underneath it all, wanting the universe we once built together to again consume me in its own power and language.

There I stood, more distinguishable from my twin brother than I had ever been in my life.

I hated every minute of it.

This is not what was supposed to happen. Camp was to be one of those I-only experiences. It was supposed to be a time when I would reach inside myself like a magician pulling a rabbit out of a hat and draw from deep within me a person completely separate from my brother. I was to come out of camp renewed, and born again like a silver-tongued gospel singer. And I was supposed to be transfixed, but not in a horrible and grotesque way. It was supposed to be more beautiful than that.

It was supposed to be much more liberating.

When I was with my brother, I was a novelty, a celebrity in the eyes of our onlookers.

Alone, I was scary and grotesque.

16.

Less than twenty-four hours before the experiment would take place, I pondered all the steps that had brought me to that bed. The path of this disease was something Bobby had not shared with me; it was a memory reserved only for me not out of selfishness, but out of protection. It was enough to know that the diagnosis came suddenly. It's the feeling you get when you hear the brakes of a car as they screech to a complete stop, and you wait in suspended silence. Impatiently awaiting those five seconds before determining whether or not it was a close call or a sudden impact.

With an AIDS diagnosis, it is always sudden impact.

In the first decade of the illness, a positive diagnosis meant a death sentence. What was certain: we were all going to die way too early. What was uncertain: exactly which of the list of horrific infections would cause it?

One pondered these things the way one ponders the final decisions of life. Will there be tubes connecting me to my final breath or will I ease the process prematurely? Will today's malady be a cancer that consumes my skin the way a tsunami consumes the coastline, or will it be pneumonia that grabs my throat and chokes me on the ready, set, go?

This was the design of my life back then, when

all the experts could offer was, *You are going to die. We just don't know exactly how.*

In those days people with this disease did not live very long, and we would drop to our knees and pray to the gods of science each and every day. Despite the fact that there was no cure.

Despite the fact our medications would eventually stop working, and we, consequently, would be faced with the same frightening questions as the generation before us. Our lives would not be as prolonged as would be the answer to this unavoidable question.

The doctors reminded me that we were not dying in the same way anymore. But while hardly anyone developed purpled skin and pneumonia, our illness would now manifest itself in other ways, as if to make a mockery of the healing process and say to us beneath its grinning teeth, *The cost of living longer is to live much more miserably.*

That is why those of us living with AIDS slowly become misshapen and disfigured in ways we would have never before imagined.

17.

When summer was over and school started, my brother and I entered middle school. The experience was entirely different from elementary school. By the sixth grade, it was clear that Bobby was the more social; this was never more evident than in gym class. I was afraid of gym class because somehow the competition was already there before we even took to the locker-room, so the pressure and expectations were threatening. And even though I was better at climbing ropes and lifting myself one peg at a time using only my hands on the peg board, these things didn't really matter to anyone but me. They were individual sports that required neither teamwork nor competitors.

Bobby, however, was the star athlete. He beat me in basketball, running, baseball, and even flag football. But by far the worst humiliation of all was yet to come.

Mr. McKay, or Mr. Mac as he was called, was a short muscular guy with a hairy chest, thick moustache and a left eye that turned slightly inward, always leaving us to question if he ever really looked directly at us when he spoke. There were jokes I could tell only with Bobby and no one else. *If Mr. Mac was cross-eyed, did he see four of us instead of two?*

But what I could not say between the laughter and the jokes was that I often wondered what it would be like to kiss him. To feel the hair of his moustache on my lips.

Instead I tried to remind myself that such thoughts do not cross one's mind in the sixth grade, at the age of eleven. Still, there was a growing comfort in knowing that these thoughts belonged to me, and for that reason alone, they were worth embracing.

Being twins meant that my brother and I had the same height and weight, making each of us the perfect wrestling opponent for the other.

Medeiros twins. On the mat. Now. That was how Mr. Mac called us when he wanted us to wrestle, and we obeyed like sycophants—Bobby, the zealous and overly eager Alpha dog twin ready to show his superiority, and me, the obedient Beta lamb twin silently going off to slaughter.

As I crept onto the mat, the other kids sat around it with their legs crossed and their voices at an audible whisper. I pretended not to hear when I heard Eugene Blackwell say to the boy next to him as he pointed to me, *That one over there is the cool one; this one here is gay.*

I held my head in shame, as if a secret that not even I knew was being exposed for all the class to hear. Up until that moment others distinguished us by two main characteristics: our grades and our popularity. I was the one who buried himself in books; Bobby was the social giant. But Eugene Blackwell distinguished us differently.

Is this what would define us from that point on?

My brother and I made it to the center of the mat where I got on my hands and knees and faced Eugene without looking him in the eye. I tried not to notice as Mr. Mac kneeled his short, hairy, muscular body next to mine, and I did not flinch when Bobby grabbed my arm with one hand and lay the other on the arch of my back. In an instant, Mr. Mac slapped his hand to the mat, gesturing for us to start with a hefty *Go!*

I could have fought my brother. Lord knows we fought all the time at home. We fought so much that once, during a fist fight, our father took us each by the hand, shouted at us to get in the car, and then drove us to the local toy store, where he bought us inflatable boxing gloves. He then drove us home, directed us to the backyard, and ordered us to inflate the gloves (mine were red, Bobby's, blue). And once we were done, we put them on, embarrassed by how ridiculous they looked. How could anyone take fighting seriously if they fought with inflated plastic balloons on their hands called *Sock'em Boppers?*

Fighting between twins takes on a meaning completely different than fighting between other siblings. For twins, fighting is not only the external embodiment of the conflict each carries within him, but it is also the result of what happens when the twinship becomes too comfortable. It was what happened when our bodies both wished to shed themselves of the comforts of our twinship and claim something far more frightening: separation, which we could only face with the courage that fighting allowed. For this reason, the anger we shared and the fists we clenched helped us get through our shared identity crisis.

But in gym class, wrestling with Bobby was different. Because in gym class, before our audience—those twisted minds that derived pleasure out of seeing twin freaks wrestle with each other—I had to allow my brother to live up to his reputation. It was the only way I could separately establish my own. Our roles were already beginning to take shape, and my weakling could not compete with his athlete, so rather than risk failure I abandoned the participation altogether.

With Mr. Mac's hand slapping the mat, I immediately collapsed under the weight of my brother's pin.

One, two, three, Mr. Mac counted, and I made no attempt to continue this battle. He leapt up and declared my brother the winner, a title he was already used to.

Deep down I suspected Mr. Mac wanted more of a show, and he threw his hands up in the air as if in resignation, the same way our father used to do whenever I struck out in Little League or failed to catch the baseball as it was thrown to me at first base. I could sense the anger and disappointment in his voice as he sucked his teeth and said, *Okay, off the mat. Now.*

Mr. Mac wanted a show. I wanted a kiss, and neither of us got what we wanted. I walked back to my place on the gymnasium floor, thinking only of Eugene Blackwell's words.

It's not that I disliked sports. And it's not that Bobby was always better at them than I was. It had more to do with the competition behind it all.

Competing against my brother meant I had to stand on my own, and I was too much a part of him to be able to do that; it would be like competing with myself. And by not competing with him, others saw us separately, for the first time in our lives.

Whether Bobby could understand that or not, he reveled in the reputation he created for himself, so I rebelled by taking an interest in anything that was not physical. We both intentionally sought separate interests.

I turned to things both artistic and analytical. I

continued to write poetry and joined the Backgammon Club, and the even less popular Math Club. Our individual identities were starting to take form.

But still there was Little League, which my brother and I always played together. I can't recall why I agreed to play another year. I think it had something to do with our father being the coach and needing more players on the team. All I really remember is that I didn't have a choice. Bobby, however, could not wait to get on the field.

Why can't you be more like your brother? our father asked.

I looked at Bobby, who was now smirking back at me. It was not the first time he said this, but it hit me as if it were. *Why can't you be more like your brother?*

This is the question that will haunt me to my final days. It went on to fill my veins and flow through my body awaiting treatment, and it will lie beside me in my grave like a wilted flower.

Why can't you be more like your brother?

Because my brother can't be more like me.

18.

Being a twin means never really being able to hide despite your numerous attempts to do so. Friends frightened me so I continued to throw myself into the seclusion of books and obscure clubs, all in an attempt to avoid the obvious reality that I would eventually be pulled into the crowd. And in the center of that crowd would stand Bobby, my twin, my doppelgänger. The one that everyone else thought I should be.

Instead, I was the one they called gay.

The two friends who did not frighten me were Mario and Ricardo de Mello. Ricardo was our age and Mario was two years older. That they were from the same island in the Azores as our grandmother gave our father a sense that in connecting with them we were somehow connecting with the part of our past that he was not able to provide. Whenever we went to their house and talked about Portugal and Providence and marijuana and girls, I wondered if Bobby ever noticed that I never wore shorts. Even on the hottest days of summer I wore my corduroys because Bobby worked out a little, and Mario and Ricardo were just naturally muscular. It was hard for me to like who my brother was becoming when looking at him reminded me of me—blue eyes I never wanted, fair skin that always burned instead of tanned, and a lanky body I could not make attractive even in my shortest shorts.

It wasn't so much that he was everything he was; it was that he was everything I never wanted to be. That was never more clear to me than in middle school. Until then, I had always been known by my middle name, Tommy. Everyone called me Tommy— everyone in school, at home, in the neighborhood, at church. So when I reached the sixth grade and switched over to a new school, the bureaucracy of that school forced me to be John. Teachers and students called me by my new name, and I unintentionally ignored them most of the time. I was labeled uncooperative. Non-responsive. Antisocial.

It first happened in English class, when Miss Greenberg pulled me aside at the end of the class and said, *I would like to see you here, in this room at 2:30.* I did not have it in me to ask why, instead, obsequious as I was, I showed up a minute early. I entered the classroom, sat at the desk where I usually sat and waited for Miss Greenberg to explain why I was there. I waited. It was 2:40, and I waited. Then 2:45, and I still waited. It wasn't until the guidance counselor passed by and saw me inside that he popped his head in and asked her, *What's he being punished for?*

Punished? Did he say "punished"? What was this punishment, and what did I do wrong to deserve it?

Oh, he likes to play games on me. He ignores me in class, pretends he doesn't hear me when I'm calling on him, so I'm playing the same game with him now.

But you never call on me, I replied. *Never.*

That's not true, John. Then the revelation hit.

I suppose one could argue that both twins are not always expected to respond when called upon, since one response is often satisfactory, and therefore tend to develop a habit of not answering directly. But this was not the case with Miss Greenberg.

The problem was much less complicated than that. The problem here was that I was never called by my first name in my life. It was a name I was not used to. But this school was big, much bigger than any other we had attended by that time, and it became instantly clear that from then on, I would either be John or I would be punished.

What I did not know at the time was that being John would eventually lead to an identity completely separate from my brother. And that in order to be myself, I needed to allow this name change to take place.

It won't happen again, Miss Greenberg. I promise.

And she released me.

And if that didn't convince me to reclaim myself, the incident that occurred the next year most certainly did. It was a day in May, a week after our birthday, the school year almost over, when I walked home from school with Ricardo.

It's a hellhole, he said about our school. *They call it a school, but it's more like a prison. I can't wait to get out.* And in some ways he was right. Our liberties were checked at the front door. Our valuables were stored in cabinets with locks that served no other purpose but to be broken and stolen. The windows had metal bars on them, and there were always doors that were locked. There was the sound of the hollow echo that followed us as we walked down the hallway from one class to another, each foot step repeating itself until we made our way to our final destination.

But for me school was also a haven that protected me, if only for a few hours, from the harsh fist of the world outside.

We met at the side door that faced the black fence by the library, as usual. Ricardo had nothing with him but the gum he was chewing; I had my backpack that held more books than I needed.

You gonna read all those books, or you just trying to look smart? He teased.

I chose not to answer. Instead I changed the subject and asked, *Where's Luis?*

I was hoping he'd say that Luis wasn't joining us; I never knew what Ricardo liked about him. Luis was a troublemaker. He stole books that he would never read and he punched teachers just because he felt like it, always in the name of what he called Puerto Rican vigilante justice.

He should be here any minute, but we can't hang around here because he is supposed to be off the school grounds, since he's gotten himself suspended again, Ricardo replied.

At that moment Luis called our names as he made his way toward us. He wore a hooded sweatshirt, hoping the hood would somehow disguise him, even though he had a walk that distinguished him from anyone that we knew, more like walking sideways than forward.

Hey, smart-ass, he greeted me as he smacked the back of my head when he finally approached.

There I was walking with a suspended junior high delinquent and the buddy who admired him. We hadn't made it more than sixty feet when they approached us, the gang of three that we all knew by face but not by name. I knew one was in class with my sister, but that was all I knew about him. But there was something about him that instilled in me a fear deeper than any I had felt up to that moment. The scar of his face, perhaps. Or maybe the angry squint of his eyes. Or the facial expression that suggested distance. Whatever it was, it immediately made me afraid. Like a dog knowing only survival, he smelled my fear and singled me out.

Get the one with the bag, was all I heard. Two held me against a fence while the other slipped his hand into a leather glove, took a roll of quarters and tightly wrapped his fingers around it, and threw the first blow to my gut.

The world at that moment moved in slow motion. I remember the scar on the left side of his face. The gray hooded sweatshirt in early summer; the white of his sneakers overshadowing the hints of green at the toes, as if he had walked silently through grass to get to me.

My backpack fell to the ground, and before I could catch my breath the second blow landed in my face and drew blood. Still held to the fence, I watched as Ricardo and Luis stepped over my bag and continued to walk home as if the assault was happening only in my mind. But the pain I felt was real as my attackers continued with my gut and my face until blood rushed from my nose and my mouth. The third punch silenced me because just before the last blow, the toughest gang member looked me in the eye and said, *This is because you came back for more.*

Came back for more? I did not understand what he meant until I arrived home, shaken and bloody. I opened the door to find my brother sitting there on a chair while Mom tended to his wounds.

Not you, too, she said. *Not you, too!*

And then it became clear, like a completed homework assignment. I was not randomly chosen to be assaulted. My cuts and bruises were there for a reason. They were there because of my twin brother, because my identity was inseparable from his.

I was being punished for looking like him.

I had no idea what Bobby did to that gang to incite such anger, but I vowed from that moment on that I would do everything possible to be as far from my brother's social circles as I could. That I would always be John. And that I would never again call myself Tommy.

From that day on I began to use my given name, a name by which the world will come to know me, a name with only four letters, with no fulcrum on which to balance the left and the right, the right and the wrong, the living and the dead.

Entire lives, I had come to learn, can hinge on just one letter.

Of course I did not know it at the time, but the discord would later embrace me and satisfy my need to be my own separate person. The jumbling back and forth between what was really my name and what I thought was my name would have its advantages, and for the first time in my life, my name would no longer be coupled with my brother's.

Being John, I would now start to become. ·

19.

In my new world, I was once again facing a competition. But unlike the competition that comes with being a twin, this was a different type of survival. The man in the room next to mine was suffering the same fate, our T-cells a competition of numbers, mostly hundreds really, where we had both started out with five. It turned out that after one year I was losing by nearly ten score. *I seem to be tolerating meds better,* he told me, smiling at his accomplishment.

(Why do I always seem to lose every competition I face?)

Out of our denial and discomfort we said that the game was over, no winners, no losers, no one left to keep score. But he and I both knew that there were no time-outs, and our numbers fell steadily like the countdown ticking of a clock. The man in the room next to mine liked to count but did not count. He was not my timekeeper, my referee, and I was not yet in overtime.

I returned to my room, and I was lying there in bed in a government-funded research institution which, for reasons I had yet to fully fathom, had an interest in keeping me alive. I was lying here in bed trying to figure out how I came to be there.

There was a dresser in the room. On this dresser in this room there was a clipboard with my name on it and a box of tissues. And there, with me and within me, flowing in and out of my veins, was the virus I called my beloved because, as with all lovers, our histories will forever be shared.

I am not alone.

We all have a story to tell. The old woman in the butcher shop who has been ordering the same cut of meat for twenty years. The boy who late at night secretly plays with his sister's doll. The man who kisses his wife to sleep and then loosens the band that stains his lonesome finger. My story involves the one I call my beloved, who had been with me for nearly five years by then, through all my highs and lows.

We all have our private histories, and my beloved and I, we are no different.

20.

Superheroes come in all shapes and sizes and children latch on to those heroes with whom they most identify. In secret, I identified with an eight-year old acrobat named Dick Grayson. Dick was the youngest of the Flying Graysons, and when his parents were killed by a gangster, he became a legal ward of a billionaire by the name of Bruce Wayne. Bruce Wayne, as everyone knows, is the alter ego of Batman. Dick was his sidekick, Robin, the Boy Wonder.

I imagined Bobby to be my own personal Batman—playboy, philanthropist, avenger of justice, and I his Robin. There was something in the vigilante justice message that caught on, and my brother and I played the roles as if they were tailor-made for us. Our parents were aware of this early on, and it was evident the Christmas when we were twelve, when they bought for us dolls to match our new identities.

Bobby, of course, was Batman, the leader of the pack (although the pack was only two). The one who sought truth and justice in everything from school principals to lemonade trucks. And I, of course, his Robin. The sensitive and trusty sidekick who stood by from the sidelines. Robin was the one who secretly wanted nothing more than to see his friend happy. He knew that without his ward, Batman could never be complete.

This is what living from the sidelines meant. And this is what I told myself whenever I took the blame for something my brother did.

The incidents were many. This time it was late spring when we sat on the porch of a house on the street next to ours. It was a childhood scene that I remember well, and at the same time, one I have a hard time believing. There were six of us, a rough and diverse lot: In addition to Luis, Mario, and Ricardo, there was Wing, who arrived from China just a couple of years earlier, always ready to discuss mathematics while at the same time clutching his nunchucks, always ready to show us the latest karate moves he learned from the movie theater down the street that showed only Bruce Lee movies.

There we were, six inner-city not-all-delinquents sitting on the porch waiting for the summer sun to tell us what to do when the lemonade truck made its way around the corner.

Yo, Wing, my brother said in his coolest voice. *Isn't that the driver who made fun of you for being Chinese?*

And before I could look up to see what was happening the five of them were hurling rocks at the truck in some strange form of solidarity. *Run, stupid!* Is all I remember my brother shouting as we all ran behind the house to jump the fence to safety.

I was never good at running fast. I was never good at throwing rocks at trucks and fighting fire with fire. And I was never good at jumping fences. And so my brother pushed me over the fence, perhaps to help me escape the men who chased us, or perhaps so he himself would not be caught. All I know is that I was lying on the cement, face scratched and bleeding, when I heard the men approach, and I got up and we all ran as fast as we could. The others before me all turned left to lose themselves among the cars in the hospital parking lot across the street. I turned right to distract our chasers, and to sacrifice myself so that my brother could get away.

Such is the way with trusty sidekicks.

Of course I got caught right away. I was thrown into the lemonade truck where two burly men showed me a gun and warned me that I would be shot if I tried to escape. Funny, but I was not scared at all, even at the sight of the gun. We knew that the guys who drove Aunt Emily's lemonade trucks were a bunch of racists, and even at that age they did not scare me.

Help us find the others, and we'll let you go, they said, offering me lemonade that I refused to drink.

You've got to be crazy, was my only reply.

At that moment my brother ran right past us. Bobby, my other me. He was even wearing the same shirt, so I was not very convincing when I told the driver that I had never seen him before in my life. Instead, the truck stopped, the driver chased my brother until he caught him, and picked him up and threw him in the truck.

This one's going to the police department, the driver said, and then set me free. I stood there in the parking lot, wondering what would happen as I watched the lime green truck drive away.

I went home, helped myself to a glass of water, and said nothing to our parents until they asked, *Where's your brother?*

And in the most nonchalant voice I could muster, I replied, *Oh, I think he was arrested.*

They looked at me quizzically, unaware that for a sidekick to be trusty, he never willingly reveals the secrets of his companion.

21.

On how to love a poz man:

Scientists will tell you several things: First, they'll say that we vary in the way we respond to outside stimuli. (They'll be thinking of how we respond to virus.) They'll say, *Some stave off the virus for a very long time; others succumb to it right away.* Say, *Better to begin HAART treatment now,* to the man in the corner who cannot fall asleep. Say, *Better to hold off on treatment so that you have options in the future,* to the man who still drives himself to work each day. Scientists will tell you several things about a poz man's response to outside stimuli.

(They'll be thinking, of course, of how he responds to virus.)

What they will not tell you, and what they will not be thinking, is that the man who shivers from the cold, thin river of ice that flows through his veins knows more than anyone else how to make love. They will not tell you that he has learned out of lacking what it means to fully receive. That each infected and dying cell that now makes up his tired, deteriorating body—from the soft, wet pillow of his hungry lip to the perfect mound of flesh just below his belly—each individual cell has learned not to turn itself away from the warmth of another man. That after an endless string of exile he has learned to respond to whatever outside stimuli offer the slightest asylum.

When you touch him—especially at the soft curve

of the shoulder where hair often refuses to grow—his skin will flutter like a featherless bird in the palm of your unsuspecting hand. You may even notice the tiny bumps flowing from his shoulder to the side of his torso, spilling onto his hip and down the inside of his leg. *I cannot begin to describe how good that feels*, he may say when you trace the path with your fingers. All you will do is touch him.

This is how a poz man responds to outside stimuli.

And when the skin that quivers just beneath your fingertips begins to feel as though it is going to explode or retreat (you won't know which) you will stroke it like a tender wound because it will seem the natural thing to do. And as you stroke it like a tender wound because it will seem the natural thing to do, his eyes will roll back into their sockets. And you will want to say, *I am here*. Want to say, *Your skin has a soul all its own*. And if you, too, are poz, you will want to say, *It's hard to tell where I end and where you begin*. But you will say nothing because words have no place in this most holy of sanctuaries, and instead, you'll allow your fingertips to find those remote places where words only intrude.

And as his eyes roll back into their sockets, they will trigger that thing within his brain that tells his head to lean all the way back as if you are bathing him with your presence. And as his eyes roll back into their sockets, his mouth will open ever so slightly, and a breath too faint to hear will escape into the silent ether and beckon you to kiss him.

And you will.

And the kiss will begin with lip against lip, and your heart will race just short of seizure. Lip against lip and you will want to burst out of your skin. Lip against lip and the walls around you will develop

their rhythm. Their own private heartbeat. Lip opening lip and tongue against impatient, unquenchable
tongue.

And scientists will not tell you what happens next,
so there is no way for you to know what to do when
his body invites you to enter him the way a city too
long silent suddenly invites sound. You will think, *All
this wonder in the palm of my hand.* Think, *He is as vast as
an open field.* Think, *To be inside him is to meld with all his
beauty and all his history and all his joy and all his pain.*

The intensity grows, and you will think only of
melding.

So you cover his mouth with your hand as you
enter him because the unspoken rule has already established itself: words only intrude. And as you enter
him, he will touch the soft curve of your shoulder
where hair often refuses to grow, and your skin will
flutter like a featherless bird in the palm of his hand.
And tiny bumps will flow from your shoulder to the
side of your torso, spilling onto your hip and down
the inside of your leg. And you will want to say, *I am
here.* Want to say, *Our skin has a soul all its own.* Want to
say, *It's hard to tell where I end and where you begin.* And
your eyes will roll back into their sockets, and your
head will lean back as if he is bathing you with his
presence, and your mouth will open ever so slightly,
and a breath too faint to hear will escape into the
silent ether.

22.

It was the year the snow fell hard, over three feet in just one day. It was the year the paint chipped from the side of the garage, and the year the neighbor spray-painted our car.

It was the year we delivered newspapers in colossal snowdrifts to over two hundred people, and brought eggs, milk, and bread to those who were homebound.

It was the year we learned about birds and bees and all those living things the church refused to talk about.

And it was the year I'd lose my childhood friend forever.

Providence, Rhode Island, in 1978 was too small a place for a gay teenager to find himself. Too many families knew each other; too few places to run to and hide. And as a twin, there was no such thing as anonymity.

These were the lessons I learned with Mario.

He was always the sexiest and most masculine of our bunch. With his strong Portuguese features of olive skin, almond eyes and dark brown hair, and his seductive smile and slightly bowed legs, he could captivate anyone he wanted. I watched him as his Adam's apple stroked the thickness of his neck, as it moved up and down with every deep burst of laughter, his lips as they parted and formed a perfect O when he whistled at the girls as they walked by, giggling. But sexier still was the way in which he would spit. He started by opening his lips slightly, as if preparing to tell a secret. Carefully placing his wet, warm tongue on his bottom lip and allowing it to rest for a moment, as if he were about to lick something—or someone—and then he lifted his head slowly, exposing the broad muscles of his neck, the pulsating jugular just below his firm, well-defined jaw bone. Then, in the blink of an eye, his tongue darted inward as his breath bolted outward, closing his eyes all the while.

I always wished I could spit like that.

I think he always knew I was gay, even before I did. I never mentioned the many times I fantasized about kissing him, and I never mentioned to anyone our last conversation. There we were, two teenagers on the south side of town, in his house, on the third floor no one ever used. I teased him about something, his baseball team losing, his girlfriend dumping him, I don't remember exactly. And I continued to tease him, because it was too telling to offer condolence, and teasing was what men did, so I thought. It was what I had learned to do.

And I teased him because I knew it would get him angry, and when he was angry he always threw himself on the person he was angry with. I teased him because I wanted to feel him.

Wrestling with Mario was like wrestling with God. There I was, prostrate, like Christ just before the first Easter, sweating as he sat on top of me. I received his weight like something that longed to be gilded— one-Mississippi, two-Mississippi—moist breath against hungry ear.

I cannot let this end, I remember thinking.

We wrestled with our bodies. We wrestled with our minds. We wrestled, and we panted, and inside my head I could hear the countdown of an imaginary referee: *one . . . two . . .* I never wanted to make it to three. I chose instead to live in that space between the second and third count, hoping it would stretch itself long and thin. Stretch itself like hot, salty taffy, while I listened only to the sounds of our breath panting together, and felt nothing but our chests rising and dropping in unison. We were, at that moment, one being, sharing one heavy, passionate breath.

This was deification, pure unadulterated worship. This was my moment of conversion. To see his rippled body inches from my weakening imagination, his torso, stomach, groin as they passed by my adoring eyes and pressed down on me, offering his host. I was no match, I knew that. Instantly he crucified me, his hands against my wrists, hard knees against soft shoulders. We panted, he with exhaustion, I with passion.

One . . . two . . .

And then everything stopped.

At that moment his eyes rejected mine. They did not let me look where I wanted to look; instead, his soul went on reserve. Our chests rose and collapsed in unison one final time. My breath picked up over here, his lips parted over there, as if failing to hold on to a whisper. He removed himself, brushed himself off and stepped back with hands held up in surrender.

You are enjoying this too much, he said, head bowed, with a trace of disgust and disappointment. Eyes still fixed on the floor that now stood between us like an entire continent of ice and snow.

We never reached the third count.

23.

I held on to my studies with the passion of a prisoner, hiding myself in my books to hide myself from my brother.

But that only lasted until the universes of our summer collided. The school year had just ended, and the days stretched themselves so long and thin that evening seemed to take forever to arrive. On this particular day it was 1:00 in the afternoon and I found myself on the corner of Broad Street and Public, pedaling my bicycle toward Roger Williams Park. That corner was always a busy intersection, and I learned to obey the traffic lights whenever I approached them. On this summer day, at this afternoon hour, the traffic light was green, and as I rode my bike through the intersection an oncoming car took a left turn in front of me, cutting me off in my path. Before I could get out of its way, I smashed into the side of the car and flipped over to the other side of the sidewalk. I remember lying there as if paralyzed, and I remember opening my eyes to see dozens of people hovering over me asking if anything was broken.

I had no idea how much time had passed between the collision and the time I opened my eyes. I picked myself up, got back on my bicycle and pedaled my way back home, unaware of the meaning of the pain in my neck. When I got home I told my mother what happened, and she took me to the emergency room at the hospital down the street. Diagnosis: whiplash.

It was then I learned that when we lift ourselves out of bed, we lift our head first. And if we fail do so, the rest of the body does not follow. I spent the next week turning to my side and pushing myself up. And as I did there was Bobby, watching and laughing from the sidelines.

Don't you even know how to ride a bike? My brother teased, completely unaware of how this story would end. *Don't you even know how to ride a bike?* He asked, the sarcasm dripping from his mouth like rotten candy.

Just wait until this happens to you, was the best response I could come up with.

Yet it sufficed, because exactly one week to the day of my accident, at the exact same time, at the exact same intersection, the exact same thing happened to him.

It was a fate waiting to happen.

I only hope it wasn't the same driver, I said to my brother as he lay bedridden, wearing my hand-me-down neck brace. *Because that would be too weird.*

When I look back at that incident, I wonder if my words were some sort of curse. *Just wait until this happens to you* implies that it will happen, sooner or later, which is not an irrational way of thinking with twins.

If my words were not a curse, the incident certainly was. This was no different from that time I was assaulted at school by that gang who first assaulted my brother, only now the order was reversed. And so as twins we carry the secret burden of knowing that whatever happens to one of us could very likely happen to the other.

Such is the way with trusty sidekicks.

24.

In the hospital room, I thought, *I fear I will lose my words when all this is over. I'm afraid that if I don't record every sound, every sight, every thought, that the experiment will fail and none of this will matter. I will be sent home as if none of this ever really happened. And the science fiction novel that is taking place right now in this universe that surrounds me will be told only in the past tense.*

But the past tense is really all we have. And so I found myself scribbling thoughts as they scampered through my mind, all in an attempt to hold on to my past because the present was so frightening, and the future as distant as a cure. I started with a poem, conjuring up those thoughts of childhood when all that mattered was being Portuguese and playing games in summer.

For me, the pleasure was in knowing that my brother and I could enjoy the same thing, though it meant something completely different to each of us. Wrestling was an act of prowess for Bobby; for me, it was something akin to public sex. For him, baseball was competition, my brother in the major league division, and me in the minor; for me, it was a way of enjoying life without him.

But football was different. Football was the sport that taught me all I needed to know about being a gay teenager. When we played football with the de Mello brothers, I was never on Mario's team.

Touch football originated in the Navy, he once said, but that didn't explain why we played it every weekend in the churchyard on the corner, Portuguese women in their shawls and cars passing by to witness the touch, referees all. And it didn't explain why week after week I found myself wanting to play, needing that touch the way summer needs children in order to feel worthwhile.

It's safer than tackle, he said, as if safety were my concern, and injury not worth the contact.

25.

That September Bobby and I entered our last year of middle school, and I found myself once again fascinated by numbers and the possibilities they contained. Like words in lines of poetry, numbers were one thing standing on their own, and something completely different when put together. Formulas were like sentences that spoke a secret language, and I felt protected and apart from others, including my brother, because I was able to speak that language so fluently. It was because of this ability to speak this odd language that I was one of only two students selected to represent our middle school in the statewide mathematics competition. The other student was a boy named Robert Correia.

My brother never noticed Robert, but I remember the day I first met him. We sat next to each other in math class, and I'm sure he noticed me as I stared shamelessly at him, admiring the tone of his skin, and how he wrote his equations, left-handed.

And, of course, he had a Portuguese name. *The Portuguese led the world in exploring new lands.* A history teacher once told our class. *They carried the secret of discovery in their blood.*

And since taking that class I always pictured myself with other Portuguese boys (despite the fair skin I inherited from my mother's side of the family); discovering new territories together and exploring unknown landscapes.

We quickly became friends; I liked him because there was a warmth I felt whenever I was around him—something I had not felt since I witnessed the solar eclipse with Curtis Jensen in the first grade. But this time with Robert things were a bit different, mainly because we were both older, and I was more aware of the feelings that began to stir inside me. I admired him the way a fan admires a movie star—with more interest than he actually deserved. And perhaps he liked me in the way that most beautiful people like their admirers; we do, after all, keep them young and timeless.

When it was announced that the two of us were the only two selected for the mathematics competition something inside me pulsated. I always enjoyed numbers—from the symmetry of our family, to the silly counting game that Miss Mora invented in the third grade that I soon mastered more than anyone else in the school, to the math puzzles featured in the next issue of Dell's *Pencil Puzzles & Word Games.* Addition and subtraction were too easy to interest me, and multiplication and division were more of a life lesson than a mathematical formula.

As a twin, I learned quickly in life what it means to multiply everything by two—shirts, pants. Grief, despair. And as a twin, I also learned quickly in life what it means to divide everything by two—Christmas presents, birthday parties. At times, even my own happiness.

So when our math teacher, Mrs. Michaelson, selected Robert and me to be the only two students in the school who would be studying pre-algebra to prepare us for the competition, I felt a sense of freedom in it all. This was about more than math. It was the beginning of a life of my own. A life where I would learn new equations to offset the doubling and the halving I had become so used to. I would begin my life with a friend Bobby did not know. Someone with whom I would take on the entire school. A new kind of sidekick.

The mathematics competition was held in mid-November at the local all-boys private school that towered on the north end of town. It was not anywhere near our school; this was evident by the houses in the two neighborhoods. In our area of South Providence the houses were either run down Victorians, abandoned after too many years of expense and neglect, or tenements, two to three families packed into one building. In northwest Providence, however, were single-family homes where lawns were carefully manicured and houses had porches and picture windows and neighbors lived thirty feet apart from each other.

Robert and I arrived that Saturday at the same time, after being dropped off by our mothers. We spent the morning taking tests. Tapping pencils and eagerly pacing ourselves, jumping back and forth between the clock on the wall and the multiple-choice options before us. When we were done that afternoon we met in the cafeteria, where we ate lunch and talked about those questions that stumped us on the test. We were then given passes to watch a football game between two teams that were easily forgettable.

Who the heck wants to watch football? Robert asked. I knew at that moment he'd be a friend forever. *Let's do something else instead.*

Something else consisted of walking under the bleachers, making our way through them like hunters on safari. And all the while I kept repeating to myself the words of my history teacher: *The Portuguese led the world in exploring new lands. They carried the secret of discovery in their blood.*

This friendship with Robert was different from my friendship with Mario and Ricardo because this was a friendship that I didn't have to share with anyone. For that, I treasured it more.

Robert and I trekked the landscape below the bleachers for hours, until the game was finally over and we made our way back to the school, where our parents waited for us to bring us back home.

Oh, by the way, he said with an air of nonchalance.

I won't be going back to school in January. My family's moving out of state. He then waved a goodbye without feeling its pain, and I stood there, struck by a type of lightning bolt, and watched as he and his mother drove off.

I walked to the car, feeling the weight of every Portuguese navigator who discovered new lands centuries ago, and the weight of all those Portuguese sailors who have done nothing ever since. And when I arrived, I saw my brother sitting in the passenger's seat with Mom behind the wheel. I crept into the back next to Bobby and pondered what I would say when he asked behind his grin, *So how was it? Tell me everything that happened.*

I missed Robert for the rest of the school year. I looked for him in the empty chair that had come to haunt Mrs. Michaelson's 2:00 math class every afternoon, Monday through Friday. And I imagined him sitting next to me on that last day of school, in the cold damp auditorium with its cracked plaster and ripped chairs as the principal of the school announced, *And this year, the award for the highest scholastic achievement among the boys of the 1979 graduating class goes to John Medeiros.*

Smartest boy. That's what we called it, but the award was both a blessing and a curse. On one hand, it was an award. On the other, it allowed me the superlative: Highest achiever. Smartest.

And it was then I learned that superlatives contradict the very nature of twins because with superlatives, there is always only one.

26.

Ninth grade is that awkward stage where we feel mature enough to reach puberty but childish enough to be afraid of it. That awkwardness is doubled with twins. At the time we entered high school, and my brother and I were kept further apart from each other than we had ever been in school. We were like lions in two separate cages.

Being kept in separate classrooms made it easier for our teachers to tell us apart, never having to worry about scolding or praising the wrong one. And though our teachers were no longer confused, such was not the case with us. In this new school, Bobby and I found ourselves confused in our new universe, which now consisted of three identical buildings, triplets, each three stories high, each connected by large hallways. Each challenging us to distinguish each building, and each floor, from the others that looked exactly like it. For the first time my brother and I were placed in separate classes with separate teachers. This meant I took courses like Spanish and Ancient History, and Bobby took French and Western Civilization. I preferred the arrangement.

Because my brother did not take Ancient History, he never had the chance to fully experience Mr. Jones, a tall version of Woody Allen, complete with horn-rimmed glasses with masking tape holding them together, plaid shirts, and khakis. In retrospect, he was a fool. He once made the mistake of interrupting a chubby Norma Hurst as she chewed her M&M's by saying, *You really don't need those, you know.* Little did he know that Norma had just been hospitalized for several months for an eating disorder, and this was the exact kind of remark that would send her right back to Butler Hospital.

And because he never took Mr. Jones' Ancient History class, my brother never got to learn the history of Ancient Rome. Did he know it is a story of twins, just like us? An ancient king named Numitor had a jealous brother named Amulius. One day, Amulius dethroned his brother, and his daughter, Rhea Silvia, was made a Vestal Virgin. This meant that she was made a priestess of the goddess Vesta and therefore forbidden to marry. It was the king's way of preserving his throne. But such rules apply only to mortals, and so the god Mars came to her in her temple, and she conceived for him twin sons, named Romulus and Remus.

When I first heard this story I wondered how Rhea Silvia could tell her two sons apart. Did she also use polish to paint one of the twin's toes? Were they dressed exactly alike, and did they do things—everything—in unison?

Legend goes on to say that as soon as they were born, Mars abandoned them in a remote location, since Amulius feared that the boys would grow up to overthrow him. Such is the way with dictators. And to prevent an overthrow, Mars placed the twins in a trough and threw it into the River Tiber, forcing them to provide for themselves.

I pictured the story of our cribs that found themselves so long ago in the center of our bedroom, when only the night before my brother and I were banished to opposite walls by our parents. And I pictured our cribs, floating, down the river.

But here is where the story of Rome really starts: soon after being abandoned, Romulus and Remus were found by a she-wolf the next day, and this she-wolf took pity on them and fed them with her milk. To complete the legend, they say that a shepherd found the twins and took them home to look after them, raising them as if they were his own. Notwithstanding fate, Romulus and Remus eventually reached adulthood and killed Amulius and reinstated their grandfather to the throne. Once they did this, they decided to found a town of their own, and they chose the place where the she-wolf nursed them. Romulus built walls on the Palatine Hill, but Remus mocked them because they were low and ineffective, leaping over them to show how silly they were. In anger, Romulus killed his mocking twin, continued to build the city anyway and named it after himself—Roma.

The story of Rome made me want to leap from my seat. Here I was, denying in every way possible the very identity that linked me to my brother, and for the first time in my life the reality hit me: our twin nature was part of a much larger history, a history capable of creating cities and entire civilizations.

History was teaching me that we belonged to a larger scheme of things.

Yet back at school, in the present day, our teachers had the strange notion that my brother and I were somehow accountable for each other in ways we thought we had left behind us. For example, one day as we were sitting in home room (the only fifteen minutes of the day that we spent together, where students were grouped alphabetically), a teacher we never met popped her head into the classroom, looked around until she noticed us, and then pointed as she smiled and said to Mr. Grant, *So you've got the twins in your class, I see. What are they like?*

You'd be amazed, he said watching me out of the corner of his eye, *Like night and day.*

What kind of place was this? All the hype about how big an institution it was, that it took itself seriously as the only public college preparatory high school in the state where 95% of the students went on to college. I anticipated discipline, control, homework assignments meant to deprive us of any social life whatsoever. Instead the teachers, like the drones of earlier years, continued to observe us like we were their experiments, their entertainment, leaving them spellbound and always trying to figure out who was who. But there was something peculiar in Mr. Grant's reply, which he made after knowing us only two weeks, something that suggested that perhaps our differences were beginning to surface at long last, and high school would somehow be the culmination of all we had struggled for.

So I held on to the school's promise that my education would matter, and I held on to the belief that this new school was a place of hope. I chose to be immersed in the reading and homework. It was with this attention to my studies that I became fascinated by Greek mythology in freshman English class. The notion of gods as humans and humans as gods became an obsession. I was drawn to the fallacies of the divine, the fine line between mortality and immortality. I felt at home with the supernatural beings who had the power to both strike awe, as we did in the faces of our teachers, and to fail, as we did with each other.

Twins helped create Roman civilization, and the same was true with Greece.

The Greek gods represented a whole new world for me, especially the story of Castor and Pollux, the *Dioscouri.*

Castor was mortal, born to Leda and King Tyndareus, and Pollux was immortal, born to Leda and Zeus. When they were grown, Castor was killed in a dispute over oxen (or was it women?), and Pollux, without his twin brother, was inconsolable. He prayed earnestly to his father that he would be allowed to die to be with his other half. But Zeus took pity on his son, and instead allowed Pollux to share his life with his brother, half of the time in Hades, the other in Olympus. This is the way they alternated their days for the rest of their lives, always together. Forever spending half their time in Heaven, and half their time in Hell.

We see Castor and Pollux even today as two bright stars in the constellation known as Gemini.

John, you, in particular, should pay attention to this story, the English teacher said to me. He would never come to know the truth and irony in his words.

27.

Memory is a trail in the woods. Sometimes winding, sometimes straight. Always leading us somewhere, though exactly where we don't always know. But that trail changes with the seasons. In summer, covered with sun, it is soft and fertile, bringing life to the flora and fauna that surround it. In autumn it is hard and brittle, littered with dead leaves that the wind has dropped—leaves that eventually decompose and become part of the trail itself. In winter it is frozen, layered with snow and footprints of the animals that have trodden it, and in springtime it is wet with rain, stirring underneath and awakening slowly from its slumber.

In other words, memory is a natural constant, but life's experiences change how we perceive it. This is especially true with twins because twins remember experiences with similar detail, except for one central and crucial fact: which twin experienced them.

And that makes all the difference.

And that is why I am able to say that it was the time of our lives when my brother and I earned the right to be called teenagers, though we already had been, four years in the making. We were seventeen years old, and we finally ended up in two separate schools; I remained in Classical High and my brother was transferred to any other high school that would accept him. At first his transfer jolted me, because I was so accustomed to feeling like two planets in the same universe at all times, one of us always orbiting the other. But at the same time I welcomed the change because it allowed me to taste true independence for the first time.

And not only was I John, but I was John with a school, and a life, apart from my brother. I was John for who John was, and not for who Bobby wasn't. I began to shape myself, to see the world around me as a world with possibilities. Alive, robust, waiting for me and me alone.

28.

During my last year of high school students began to notice I was gay even before I did. My brother avoided me because of what that meant for him, and what role it played in his own personal quest for identity. If it is true that as twins we are always a part of the other's identity, then how would my being gay fit into my brother's natural plan? What if I were gay? What would that make him?

My brother took to the streets and hung out with his friends more than his own family. Never did I mention the times I saw him in the alleys, knowing he was up to something but not knowing what it was, exactly. By this time our parents bought the house we lived in, and we moved upstairs so we would each, for the first time in our lives, have our own separate bedrooms.

This was supposed to be big news. This was supposed to be the first time we would sleep separately from each other, no longer like fetuses attached to the same womb. I doubt anyone else saw any significance in this at all.

I'm gonna paint my room blue, I said, waiting for my brother's response.

Yeah, who cares? He said, shutting the door behind him.

Then one day, after avoiding me for several months, my brother silently eased himself into my room, slithering in like something wet, his chin digging into his chest, a steady flow of tears scarring his face. He approached me, shaking with a fear I had never seen before. *I'm scared*, he whispered. *Real scared.*

What is it? I asked, vowing not to tell anyone.

I don't know. I did some drugs, okay?! I took a hit of mescaline, he said. *Only this time it doesn't feel like it usually does. This time everything inside me feels like it's vibrating.* My brother sat on the bed and trembled as I watched the drug take its effect.

Have you told Mom and Dad? I asked. And before he could answer I went on. *Of course we have to tell them, but don't worry, I'll be here if they get upset.* There he was, telling me for the first time in my life that he needed me, that after several months of separation, regardless of who I was and what I was becoming, he was asking me to be part of the solution. How hard it must have been for him to need me at that moment while at the same time feeling the need to reject me.

I was used to this dichotomy, but I never thought that he was feeling the same struggle.

We told our parents and to our surprise they did not get upset. Safety was their priority, so they took Bobby to the hospital down the street. Though the doctors did not pump his stomach to rid him of any toxins, the very threat of it was a wakeup call for him. My brother was hurt and scared, and I shared his pain and fear.

For the next two weeks I watched him battle the depression that followed. Keeping an eye on him constantly, twenty-four hours a day, and throughout it all I witnessed my own heavy breathing. My own anxious sweat and elevated heartbeat. Beyond my brother I saw nothing but clouds, graying in their sullenness, wrapping themselves around him and taking him away from me and banishing him to a world I knew nothing about.

It was a fear that started in my stomach and worked its way throughout my entire body. All our lives we dressed for school together; ate the same meals together; played the same games together; and fought the same fights together. And despite the discomfort and the rivalry, I found myself wanting all of those things all over again.

But I would be lying if I did not say that I also despised him when he did not sleep at night, when he instead glared at the moon every evening sweating out his depression while talking about the futility of life. I was not as strong as he needed me to be, but still he kept asking for more. In his own pain and fear he held on to me, and there was no way I could burden him with mine.

Such is the way with trusty sidekicks, I reminded myself with a hint of irony. If truth be told, unlike the trusty sidekick, I did not know how to react to the sudden shift in our universe. My brother now needed me. What would it be like for Robin to suddenly lead Batman?

One night, when no one was around I whispered to Bobby, *Do you realize that this is the first time in our lives I can remember you actually needing me?*

No it's not, he said. *It's just the first time I told you.*

29.

Eyes closed.

In that room I told time by the sound of the crickets singing their warning songs to me, the pig ready for the slaughter. A pig not of plastic on a toy farm from childhood, but antiseptic white, like the flag I waved to the virus marching across my body like an army of one. Pig of science, and drugs pretty like gumdrops.

I lived not in the days of scalpels and Sodium pentathol blowing into my veins like helium into a balloon, but of witch doctors and medicine men taking lives, trekking miles across the western world to throw something worthwhile into my veins, the cure-all, the magic whose name no one knows.

I was told my skin may rash or get bubbly.

Or nothing.

And I curled myself up like a paranoiac, rocking back and forth on my own hinges, clinging to myself like a hamster, only bigger.

But this was not how it was supposed to happen. This was not the design and definition of the second of two twins, the one who got to learn from the mistakes of the other. The one who was not supposed to make mistakes on his own. Whether I wanted to or not, I was supposed to follow in my brother's footsteps. All that happened to me was supposed to have happened to him first. Wasn't that only fair with identical twins? Wasn't that supposed to be the pattern of our scientific and calculated lives?

I passed the room of a man in a chair and read the name temporarily scribbled in marker—Stephen Joyce. At first I remarked on how temporary everything seemed in this permanent institution on the hill. Even names were delible and forgotten over time.

Disease and death are the only permanents here, I thought aloud. *Everything else is written in erasable marker.*

And then I pondered his name: Joyce. Like the Irish writer I studied in high school, this Mr. Joyce was opening my eyes to a world I was not yet prepared to face alone. *Joyce,* I said to myself, nodding, remembering being told about the library upstairs. I figured I could use a dose of Joyce about then so I asked the nurse for a pass to the patient library located three flights up and I was given one, along with a reminder to return within the hour so the nurses could record my vital signs.

The library was much smaller than I thought it would be, given the size of the campus. Literature, books for leisure, magazines—there were no science journals in this small universe of books. Just the things that are supposed to help us forget where we were. Fortunately, they had the book I was looking for, so I checked it out and returned to my room.

Total time: sixteen minutes.

I first read *A Portrait of the Artist as a Young Man* in high school, after Bobby left at the end of our sophomore year. I remember falling in love with Joyce's writing after reading the book's very first paragraph:

> Once upon a time and a very good time
> it was there was a moocow coming down
> along the road and this moocow that

was coming down along the road met a
nicens little boy named baby tuckoo. . . .

Never before had I read prose that was so poetic.
There was a freedom in his language, a freedom I
would come to embrace and identify with because
it was the first time in my life when I attended school
without my brother. The world of education was
opened to me in a way it had never been opened
before. No one would ever know how liberating that
time was for me. I was released in a way I'd never been
released before, and like Joyce's protagonist, Stephen
Daedelus, as an artist and as a person, I was beginning to come out of some self-made casing and emerge
as something new.

Ding dong! The castle bell!
Farewell, my mother!
Bury me in the old churchyard
Beside my eldest brother.

Even then, a decade after reading them for the first time, Joyce's words
struck me hard as an axe and made sense in ways I was still only beginning to understand.

Chapter three, and Joyce's character has just committed the "first violent sin" of lust. With it, the chain
reaction of gluttony and laziness. Ultimately, the inability to pray in that traditional, Catholic sort of way.

What drew me to Joyce was his character's devo-
tion to beauty, which Stephen came to worship over
the Catholicism that had ruled his life. I identified
with the internal struggles of Joyce's alter ego, with
his need to question that which we are told we must
believe. And I identified with his prayers, and his

rejection of creed, choosing instead to pray in his own
way for those things he loves.

There, in that hospital bed that had become my home away from home, I found myself praying in the way Joyce taught me to pray: for my brother and for all the things that had come between us from the day we were born to that exact moment in our mutual but separate lives.

I prayed for the trees we'd never climb again.

I prayed for the Little League games we'd never play.

I prayed for the amusement park rides and the matching clothes, and the times we'd listened to albums on our bed, and for campfires and footballs and trading cards in the alley.

I prayed for all of the things that had become lost along our path.

The path of the artist is the worship of beauty and
its truth. This is the line Joyce asks us to walk, that
which asks us to find beauty in the things around
us, while at the same time revering the divine power
behind it.

This has become my religion.

30.

After I graduated from high school I worked for a year before attending college. That year off was a critical one. It helped me discover who I was and what it was I was hiding from. I was nineteen years old, and I had my first consensual sexual encounter with another man. The experience was beautiful, natural, unprecedented—the way it should be.

I attended a concert in downtown Providence. I don't remember who performed, but I do remember walking home afterward. A blue Dodge Colt approached me shortly after the show and pulled up to the curb. It waited a few moments for me to walk ahead and then pulled up to the curb again.

I was not frightened or threatened in any way. Instead I welcomed the exchange as if it were a game, and we played it for a while before the man inside rolled down his window and said with a smile that accented his already handsome face, *I recognize you from the neighborhood.*

I had noticed him, too, over the past few weeks. He was a quiet man in his late twenties, slightly balding with a thick moustache and warm brown eyes. He wore a plaid shirt with the sleeves rolled up just enough to expose the hairy forearms I always found attractive in men. The aura he exuded was one of complete trust and humility.

I live just up the street, he told me. He was right in saying it was close by, so I accepted when he offered to give me a ride home. I really don't know why I accepted the offer, but I did. Perhaps it was that I sensed something friendly and unthreatening about him. Perhaps I knew that he and I shared more than what appeared on the surface. I cannot explain it any other way than to say it just felt natural.

On the ride home I learned his name was Anthony, that he was Italian and a mechanic by trade. We also went to the same high school, though he graduated several years before I did. Back then it was not unusual for me to stay out late, so when my newly discovered neighbor invited me to his place for a beer and to watch television, to *get to know each other better* as he put it, I accepted the offer.

We drank Sam Adams and watched *The Tonight Show* with Johnny Carson, and I peered out of the corner of my eye as he laughed at Johnny's jokes and smiled at me to make sure I was having a good time. There was something charming yet enticing in his laughter, a strange combination of breath and moan. He must have known I admired it because not much later he approached me from behind and kissed my neck.

I thought I'd be afraid, perhaps push away this gentle man who now had some sort of control over me. But I did not. Instead I trusted him with my innocence. I fell under his spell and took him in. Took in the scent of musk and beer, the feel of his body as it hardened against mine. The sounds of his breathing and his laughing as both grew softer and slower.

Let's go to the bedroom, he said, and I consented. There we shared our curiosity and our loneliness, all to the quiet glow of the TV light and the sounds of muffled laughter. I trusted him, somehow knowing he would save me from all the things I was running from: the sneers of others, the loss of respect from my brother. The toxins in the Rhode Island air.

My curious and uncertain self.

At the end of the evening he drove me home, which was just four blocks away. He kissed my neck and held my head to his chest and squeezed me to the point where I could not tell if it was his heart beating or mine.

Thank you for a beautiful evening, was all he said. There was no need for anything else.

That night Anthony was a fountain, and I reveled in the bath. I knew at that moment my life was changed forever, and whatever journey I was on, there was no turning back.

31.

Bobby graduated from high school a year after I did. He then took a
year off from high school before deciding which school he ultimately
wanted to be his last. His grades were poor not because he was a bad
student, but because knowledge came quickly to him and he easily grew
bored.

Deep down I admired that about him.

On a blistering Saturday in June 1984, my plan was to spend a few
hours at the beach in Newport with a friend, head home to shower and
change, and then make it to the auditorium hall at 5:00 p.m. to attend
Bobby's graduation. The beach was extraordinarily hot that day. I
jumped in the water to cool myself off, and then ran to my blanket to
soak up not only the sun but a really good book I had just started to
read.

And then I fell asleep.

What turned out to be a few hours ended up being closer to six.
When I woke up the sun was blinding, and my face felt like it was on
fire. Everything I looked at seemed to glow. *We need to leave!* I told my
friend. *I need to get home and then to my brother's graduation.*

We rushed to pack our things and ran as fast as we could to my
friend's car. She sped on the way home, which I secretly appreciated,
and dropped me off at my home in thirty minutes. It was impressive
that I got there so soon, though it was way too late to shower as I had
intended. Instead I threw on some jeans and a button-down shirt, took
a bus downtown and walked the twenty-minute walk to the auditorium
hall. I arrived only a few minutes late.

Reconstructed in the late 1960s in what once was a Protestant Church,
the Bishop McVinney Memorial Auditorium was a seven-hundred-and-
fifty-seat public auditorium where a number of events took place each

year, including high school graduation ceremonies. On this particular day the auditorium was packed to the gills, and the air circulation was poor. I sweated as I waited impatiently for the announcer to call the names of each graduate alphabetically. *At the pace he's going I'm going to pass out before he gets to the M's*, I said to myself. Somewhere in the mid-C's I ran to the lobby and found the bathroom and threw water on my face. I looked at myself in the mirror and saw myself for the first time since that morning. I could feel myself getting redder and redder by the minute.

I returned to my seat early enough to find the announcer still reading out names. *Great. He's only on the L's. Just a few more minutes*, I told myself, *and then we'll be done*. Not soon enough he called out Bobby's name, and I stood to my feet and applauded as loud as I could, completely unaware of the others sitting quietly beside me. *Go Bobby!* I shouted in case my clapping was not loud enough. My body burst with pride.

He made it. He actually made it. And I could not have been prouder for him than I was at that moment. I was also shaking and felt like I was going to faint, so I waited outside to meet up with him. Outside the air was hot but it was not stuffy. Bobby greeted me about fifteen minutes later and we embraced. We had not done that for a long, long time.

What are you going to do now? I asked him. *I'm going to hang out with some friends to celebrate*, he said. *You're welcome to join us.*

I wanted to, but at the same time I felt myself getting dizzier and dizzier with each passing moment. *Thanks*, I said. *But I think I'm going to head home; I'm not feeling so good. Let's talk tomorrow*, I said. And with that I walked toward downtown. He nodded as if to agree with my diagnosis.

For some reason the bus never came, so instead of waiting any further I walked home. The entire walk took about ninety minutes, and the moment I walked in the door I collapsed in a chair in the living room. My body was now radiating so much heat my clothes began to suffocate me. I ran to the bathroom to take them off and to jump in the shower to cool off. But when I took off my pants what I saw astonished me. My legs were completely blue. The heat emanated from my body so much that the dye from my jeans bled on to my legs. I knew then something was wrong. Mom took me immediately to the hospital down the street, where the doctors told me I had second degree burns on my body from falling asleep at the beach. *You're not going to be able to even move for a few days*, they warned.

They were right, though a few days turned into ten.

The next day when I spoke to Bobby on the phone, I chuckled when he said, *Wait. You went to my graduation with second degree burns? Damn, man. It wasn't that exciting!* And then with all the sincerity he could muster at the moment, he added, *Seriously. I'm happy you were there. It meant a lot to me.*

And at that moment, the burns and the scars I was told would stay with me forever seemed worthwhile.

At first I didn't notice when my brother started attending church several months later; he hadn't gone since we were children. Now Bobby had found God in a Conservative Baptist church. He told me that going to this church was a rebellious act, since we were raised on the belief that we should never leave the Catholic Church, even though we could not find God hidden between the lines of the missal.

I think the Baptists were good for him. They helped steer him away from the crime and drugs that had become his world. I respected my brother's choice for this church, even when he teased me and told me I should visit it sometime because I needed more friends in my life.

Look what it's done for me, Tommy, he said as if popping out from behind a magician's curtain. *For the first time in my life, I feel like I belong to something larger. And I feel absolutely free.*

The church helped Bobby understand his place in the world. It showed him how to take the focus off himself and to see others around him. With his church I noticed how he became more aware of others in the neighborhood, more connected to the needs of those around him. The transformation was palpable.

Why don't you join me? He asked one day. I was skeptical, but I also trusted the changes I saw in him. I thought, perhaps if he could change, I could change, too. Without telling him why, I accepted his invitation.

I had no concept of evangelism at the time, so I did not suspect that this is what was happening. Instead I grew to like the Conservative Baptist Church, which encouraged us to bring our own Bibles with us to worship service, and to ask questions when the minister preached something we did not understand.

This way of getting to know God was a rejection of creed. It was unorthodox and we welcomed the challenge because of its newness, and its potential power.

It didn't take long for Bobby to announce his desire to be baptized as an adult. *Infant baptism meant nothing to me*, my brother said. *I didn't even have a choice.* Shedding all I was taught to believe by the Catholic Church, the argument made sense to me.

Baptists call it *full body immersion*, and that is exactly what it was. There stood my brother, angelic in his white robe, walking down the flight of steps that took him into a pool of water where the minister waited as the congregation viewed from their seats. Pastor Joe read from the Bible and shared words about the meaning of baptism, reminding us that in the Baptist church, water baptism was merely a symbol of the spiritual baptism happening inside, and therefore served as a testimony. *Witness* was the term he used for those in attendance. He held my brother by the hands, asked him to bend his knees as he leaned back, and pushed my brother completely underwater.

The entire event took just over five minutes, but the effect lasted a lifetime. In amazement I watched Bobby as he was dipped into a pool of water to show us what was happening inside him.

Full body immersion.

I sat in awe as I tried to gauge what was happening inside *me*. Something stirred within me. Here was my twin brother, claiming a part of himself that was not a part of me and I sat watching humbly from the sidelines. He was becoming a part of us that I did not share, literally plunging himself into a new uncharted world.

And suddenly mine felt very empty.

Throughout it all, I was proud of what my brother did but at the same time I was scared for him and was scared for us. The baptism found me shaking slightly, the same way I did when he came home after his bad mescaline trip. There was the same heaviness in my breath. The same anxiety and sweat and elevated heartbeat. The same feeling that I was losing him to an entirely different world once again.

And though I agreed to my own baptism six months later, all this was in complete contrast to what was happening inside me. Several days before my baptism, I drove by Anthony's house. I'm not exactly sure what I was looking for. Confirmation? An attempt to keep one foot in his world, and another in this new one? I cannot really say for sure. All I remember is that when I drove past his place, I noticed his car was gone from the driveway and a FOR RENT sign was posted in the window of his apartment. My world stopped for that moment, and I allowed myself to feel its pain.

The pain of never before having anyone take an interest in me and in my body (with the unforgivable exception, of course, of Uncle Manny).

The pain of knowing that, before Anthony, people were only interested in me as an extension of my brother, or because I satisfied some strange freakish fascination of theirs.

The pain in meeting a man named Anthony, in gazing at the ceiling above us, nervous toe tapping against a silent bedpost. I lay there tapping and abstracting. *I like the flavor of your body*, this is what he told me. *I like the flavor of your body.* But my body had no flavor. My body was not special. It was nothing in particular. Not made of salt nor anything sweet. But one night, according to this man, my body had flavor. How is it that a body can have flavor? If it is washed with a secret tincture, does it become a treat? Or is it something more natural, like an accent, or a hair color? Perhaps each person has their own flavor, and when two people of the same flavor unite, that new combined flavor, a flavor alloy that grows and flourishes and makes itself known. Perhaps it was not the flavor of my body at all, but the flavor of his. Or a strange combination of the two. I do not know. All I know is that this man, a man not my peer but of a similar profile, this man liked the flavor of my body. And I remember thinking, the flavor of my body will become a second layer of skin. And that second layer of skin will cover each inch of my being. And each inch of my being, fully flavorful, will wait for his mouth once more.

But I believed deep down that this baptism would wash away that layer of skin, cleanse my body of the thought of his mouth on mine. With this baptism I washed myself. And I washed until the flavor of my body was completely wiped away. I blanched myself in despair. I erased all pigment in my skin.

I felt as though I would be forever bland, both inside and out, never flavorful again. Safe.

32.

Halfway through Joyce it became painfully clear that I couldn't read any more. I could no longer ignore the fact that each room along the fluorescent hospital corridor had about it an aura of abandonment. The doors seemed as if they should have been labeled not with patients' names but with eerie inscriptions: Shame. Suffering. Neglect. Nobody Cares Where I Am.

And why was I afraid, with all those experts surrounding me? I should have felt protected and in the best of care. Had I become afraid of the unknown? Wasn't I Portuguese, born of the courage of navigators? After all, it was Pessoa, Portugal's poet, who once wrote,

> we get along so well together
> in the company of every thing
> we never think of one another,
> but live together, the two of us,
> with an intimate understanding
> like the right hand with the left.

Later that night I fell asleep and I dreamed of a new world. And in my world I was sixteen and I was holding a peanut butter and jelly sandwich. And somewhere between the time I started eating my peanut butter and jelly sandwich and the time I got up to leave, a man in shorts approached me and ask if I had the time. When I looked at my wrist, which had no watch, and told him *I do not have the time*, he looked at my crotch while rubbing his own and asked me, *Are you sure you don't have the time?*

I looked around me and everything stood still. The children in the playground paused in mid-flight. The lovers under the trees in mid-kiss, the man with the dog in mid-walk, the set of twin baby boys in mid-scream, the woman on a bicycle in mid-pedal, the girl with an ice cream cone in mid-lick, the family having a picnic in mid-bite.

Yet my sandwich was all gone, and the man in shorts was still looking at my crotch and asking, *Are you sure you don't have the time?*

I was not sure.

I awoke. The world awaited my answer, and still I was not sure.

33.

Coming Out: Part One. To hide. To whisper. To outline your-self like a murder victim. To erase a chalk mark in the rain. To change the topic of conversation. To rewrite a story untold.

I wasn't expecting Andrés to happen. He just did, and I took him in the way a drought takes in the rain. If anyone were to ask me how it happened, I could not say exactly because the entire incident caught me by surprise. In an instant I was drawn to him and found myself studying him the way a child studies a magician. Nothing in this sleeve. Nothing in that one. And then, at the moment of least expectation, everything in my world seemed to shatter all at once, leaving bits and pieces of my life scattered about like crumbs of bread—some on the summer grass where we made love for the first time, some backstage of the university theater where we kissed each other when no one else was looking, and some in the pews of the Catholic Center where I asked God daily to love me regardless of what was happening inside me.

What I remember most was this: I was a freshman at the University of Rhode Island. Now Bobby was married to the girl he had been dating when he started going to church, and I was surrounded by an entire universe of people who did not know me as an extension of my twin. I was cast into that universe without fear. I was baptized. God was with me. And most importantly, I was free. My brother was right when he told me the church would give me freedom I had not previously known.

It was as though the membrane that surrounded my identity was finally beginning to split open.

So there I was, sitting in poetry class and discovering words and voices I had never heard before. Most of the students were less interested in poetry, being there only to satisfy their basic course requirements. *All incoming students are required to take at least three courses in English literature regardless of their major* the course catalog reminded us. Poetry 101 was one of the more popular. One day in class, when I wasn't paying very much attention, the instructor asked for a volunteer to read aloud. That volunteer was Andrés.

I listened to him as he read the poem aloud and the music sounded fresh and new. I listened as the words danced from his mouth to the back of my neck and lingered in my inner ear and I nodded. I listened to him read with a fervor and a desire and a passion as he tasted every word, letting the endless string of vowels and consonants roll upon his tongue before releasing them to the hungry audience that was me.

It was as though there was no one else in that classroom except the two of us. As he read I slowly looked back to see him, to somehow put a face with the voice that had already caught my attention. I looked back, and there he sat tall and slender, his skin, a dark olive tone. He wore an oversized cotton shirt with khaki pants and sandals left over from a previous generation, and he had a mole on his left cheek that looked like a round black raisin.

A flaw that only added to his beauty.

His hair, shoulder length, shiny black and parted in the middle hung over his eyes, and every now and then as he read, he would run his fingers through it, carefully placing it behind his ear like a schoolgirl. And when he did this, his face revealed more about his mystery: the rugged jawbone, sharp and defined with just a hint of stubble, and lips that moved ever so quickly as his voice floated across the words on the page.

He read those words with a South American accent, and the sounds he made were lovely. Not the harsh and glottal sounds I'd come to associate with most Latin accents, but soft and fricative, almost like Portuguese, lasting for as long as his breath would hold the sound. Sounds like *shhhhh* and *sssss* hissing from inside those fantastic lips.

And as he read his hands flailed, showing me that he was feeling the poetry on the page, not just reading it. Some students in the class giggled. Others simply rolled their eyes and looked away. But I sat transfixed, as if I were somehow bolted to my desk, completely unable to move.

When he finished reading, he looked up, caught me studying him and smiled a warm smile in that way an actor on stage might smile when seeing a familiar face in the crowd applaud him for his performance. I must have given myself away at that moment. I must have shown that I was somehow lost in his eyes that looked up at me like two black chestnuts, one of them taking a moment to wink before looking away.

I turned my gaze back at my book, thinking only of him and nothing else.

At the end of class he approached me. He was neither shy nor reserved. Instead he approached me, knowing how the conversation, and the rest of our semester, would turn out.

Hello, he said. *I'm Andrés. Andrés Castillo.*

I repeated his name to him in the same accent in which he delivered it, pronouncing the double *l* not as a *y* as they taught me in Spanish class, but as the *zs* sound in Zsa Zsa Gabor. *Nice to meet you, Andrés Castillo. I'm John.*

Ah. You speak Spanish, then, no? How else would you know how to pronounce my name so well?

I do. It's one of my majors.

And from that moment on two worlds opened themselves up to us. We had the poetry of the English world, clever with words and less emotive. And we had the poetry of the Spanish world, full of passion and emotion and vibrant with sound and image. These two worlds became our own, and together they came to represent the relationship that would later develop between us. A relationship full of words and emotion, neither limited to just one language. A relationship where conversations didn't happen without our senses being heightened. A relationship full of passion and the need and inability to contain it.

In just a few short weeks, Andrés and I spent as much time together as we possibly could. We took walks together. We read poetry together. We talked in two languages of God and religion—I, the Christian, he, the atheist. We sang songs of Joan Baez, Violeta Parra, and Mercedes Sosa, and we spoke on the phone for hours after we ate dinner. Our lives folded into each other snugly hand in glove. So it was no wonder and only natural that we would eventually find ourselves wrapped in each other's arms one evening in early spring.

What's happening? I asked.

I think we're falling in love, was his reply. *But let's not say another word. Let's just let it happen instead, okay?*

What I did not tell him is that, though I made love with him I did not love him. Instead, I loved what he was teaching me about myself. Making love with him was the culmination of separation from my brother. Andrés took interest in me. Andrés wanted to be with me. He enjoyed me and he loved me without even knowing my brother existed. I would look back on my time with Andrés not as something wrong and shameful, but as something unique and individual. Alone in a world without my twin meant I could share the beauty Andrés represented without questioning what it meant. Or why.

And that piety was something I could call my own. Andrés was the very first person I knew who took an interest not only in my body, but also my mind. He offered himself to me in the way I offered myself to him: through words and through beauty. This moment of independence was vital and so it had to happen in order for me to develop. But it was also frightening because it meant I could never share this experience with my brother. It was not like I could easily say, *Let me tell you what I learned today.*

This was very different because I was finally embracing what it meant to be gay. Sex with Anthony did not have a chance to spill over into emotion. Sex with Andrés did, and that made all the difference.

Andrés and I would continue to share our thoughts and our mutual admiration for each other for the rest of the semester, and every time we did, I felt bad for him because I knew I did not love him. If truth be told, I did not know how to love him, so what I felt for him was a type of admiration and gratitude. I was not even aware of my own self at this stage in my life, so how could I possibly share that self with another person? He was a free spirit, the type of lover most people fantasize about, and I admired that about him. But I needed him to understand the inner struggle I had in coming to terms with my homosexuality. I struggled with how to love another man, paralyzed by how I would find ways to embrace my identity, something that my religion had taught me was so unnatural. Andres sensed as much, so he was not surprised when one night, near the end of the semester, after making love with him in the early summer grass, I told him, *We cannot do that ever again.*

As consolation I threw myself into confessional after confessional and bathed myself in the words of the Gospel so that I might ignore the feelings inside my body that kept calling me back to him.

34.

When Bobby got married to his high school sweetheart, Sonya, I was just starting my sophomore year in college. I drove back home to attend the wedding. I remember the day he asked me to be his best man. I was incredulous about why he would ask me instead of any of his friends who were closer to him. I knew my brother loved me, but I did not know he liked me enough to ask me to be his best man.

We turned heads that day. Without having seen each other in months, Bobby and I had identical hair styles that day, and we had trimmed our moustaches and beards the exact same way. We were more identical than we'd ever appeared before as adults. Everyone, including the bride, was confused, and we took in that confusion just like we did when we were in elementary school, loving every minute of it.

Bobby and Sonya met in high school and attended the same church together. I had attended several times, but had not fully committed myself to their church because of my internal struggle. The struggle was a triangle. At one vertex stood God, a ringing voice in my head. At the second stood my sexuality, with a voice indistinguishable from God's. And at the third stood my twin brother, the voice I'd known the longest.

And the struggle lasted a year before I finally came to terms with what it means to be gay, and I accepted the identity and all that came with it. I told friends from college who claimed they never knew and lost many of them as a result. I told members of our church and was shunned by the very people who accepted me just a few years earlier. And throughout it all, with our shared friends and acquaintances, I could feel myself slipping further and further away from my brother, who seemed to take my homosexuality as a personal affront.

The strength I had to finally face my homosexuality came in the form of Daniel, an artist who captured the world around him in illustrations and collages. He was short—five feet, eight inches—with dark brown eyes and a thick brown moustache, his head and jaw more square than round. His laughter always deep from the belly.

In retrospect, it's hard to imagine what life was like all those years ago even though we both lived it, Daniel and I. Those years when we lived with lunch bags as lampshades and breakfast for dinner once a week. We learned the more rudimentary facts of living, like how to stay warm as we drove to Connecticut at Christmas, with the car windows smashed in and duct tape for locks. Or how to feed the cat while we were away, and how to make sure we always managed to have one anniversary card for the other waiting in the mail.

Anniversaries were different for us back then. *Today marks the day you first kissed me,* I wrote. *And today we celebrate that day we had our first date.*

We celebrated everything, he and I. It was Friday, so we drank a toast. We lost electricity in the middle of a thunderstorm, so we slept on the back porch with a flashlight. It was the first day of autumn, so we went for a long drive, pointing out leaves as we headed west on Route 44. It was springtime, so we picked wildflowers and brought them back to the apartment, where he spent the afternoon drawing them while I wrote poems to accompany his art.

Our priorities were different back then. What mattered most were the Joni Mitchell albums, the open windows on summer afternoons, and just enough smoke to enjoy them both. We knew how to live that life. We knew how to live those days when weekends presented themselves in the middle of the week and guests never arrived unannounced.

We knew how to live without ever hurting others.

We knew, simply, how to live, Daniel and I.

And we lived as we lived for three years, and during that time I learned more about myself and more about love than I had ever imagined I could. From the chilly October evening when we shared rings and vows in the bathtub of a candlelit bathroom, to the evenings spent on a mattress on the living room floor eating Chinese food and watching movies all weekend long on a rented VCR, to the conversations that lasted until two in the morning.

I don't mind the terms "gay" or "fag," but I prefer "queer," he said to me one day and I repeated to myself with a wine glass in hand, *I'm queer, I'm queer, I'm queer,* as if speaking the words for the first time. Repeating them, I embraced them with a sense of freedom to it all.

I was queer.

And I was in love. And it was a simple love where nothing else mattered in the world. We met when I was completing my sophomore year of college, just before I was headed off to work for the summer in Connecticut as a camp counselor. *Write me,* he said with a hint of despair and disinterest, as if I would not.

But I did. I wrote him poems about men on the open seas and poems about boys, star gazing. And I wrote about trees bending eastward, and about the body crumbling like a broken monument when separated from the body it loves. And I wrote about loss before it ever happened. I wrote him all these things because with him there was an energy that allowed my words to spill over without fear of picking them up.

We were both artists, after all, and when two artists are in love, nothing else matters.

He drove the hundred miles to Connecticut, often without notice, and I met him in the woods outside the camp where I worked and we made love in the summer night, the stars our only witness. He sent me packages in the mail, songs he composed for the recorder on cassette. And I wrote words to his music, and he put music to my words.

And for three years nothing would disturb that harmony.

It was the kind of love that yearned to be known. The kind I wanted to share with my brother, the happiness I finally found. But I told him nothing, afraid he would see me as careless, or immature, or unable to understand the responsibilities of love, which had become for him his reason for marriage.

I knew love as beauty of the senses, and it came only in the form of a man. My brother knew love only in the context of God and family and holy union.

We had finally become two separate selves, and I was afraid to reveal mine, afraid of the judgment and the failure I would later feel. As in gym class so many years ago, it was as though our roles had already taken shape, and rather than risk failure I abandoned my brother altogether.

It took one year with Daniel for me to build the confidence in myself to come out to my brother and to the rest of the family.

I remember the scene distinctly: there we were, the entire family sitting in my parents' living room waiting for me to deliver my news. Bobby sat furthest away, though I wanted him right next to me. I knew that what I was about to say was difficult, and he made it only more so by watching me from across the room the way a judge watches a witness.

I'm gay, I said. *That's what you've all been waiting to hear. I'm gay.* And I watched the family, as if in slow motion.

Scene one: My mother noticed the ring on my finger and left the room screaming, *What's that on his finger?! What's that on his finger?!* We wouldn't see her again for the rest of the night.

Scene two: My father looked up from his book and replied with a confused look on his face and the scarcest of words: *How do you know you're gay? You haven't really dated many girls.*

Scene three: My sister told me that she did not want me near her children, *Just in case you have AIDS,* she said.

Scene four: My other sister, surprisingly, simply said, *I don't care,* and she really didn't. She left the room and this was support.

Scene five: My brother's was the reaction I watched for. He was the one who best knew me all these years. He was the one others accidentally referred to as *the gay one.* He was the one who knew that God, our God, the God we both believed in, would not rebuke me. Or so I thought. I waited for him to collect his thoughts. I examined him closely like a mind reader as he contemplated the words he was going to say. We both knew each word mattered at this moment. Bobby finally looked at me with an unconvincing smile and a hint of disgust as if I were a cracked mirror and said, *You do know that's something that you can sacrifice to God, don't you?*

I said nothing. He added, *I cannot support you, if that's what you want. There's no way I can support you because what you are doing is wrong.*

I did not remind him that I was not trying to talk about anything I was *doing,* and that I was trying to talk about what I was *being.* I was not asking for debate and I don't think that I was even asking for his support. Perhaps I just wanted my brother to know that all the rumors he had heard about me over the years had actually been true. Perhaps I wanted to provide him with the correct answer the next time his friends asked him if I was gay.

I grabbed my jacket and left the house. He followed me and said, *Can we talk about this more in my car?* I don't know why I agreed, but I did, and once there he started the car, turned off the radio and said with an earnest nod, *Look, if I were sitting on the street corner getting high, it would be your Christian duty to tell me that what I am doing is wrong, right? So, when you tell me you're gay, it's my Christian duty to tell you that being gay is wrong, understand?*

This was the new Bobby. Not the Bobby shooting BB guns at passersby and finding himself, once again, in the backseat of a Providence Police patrol car. And not the Bobby overdosing on drugs, being threatened with stomach pumps by an emergency room physician. This was Bobby of the church. Bobby the Enlightened who has been washed clean by the blood of his newfound Christ so well that everything else looks like stain to him. I tried to like this Bobby.

And what would be your brotherly duty? I asked.

My brother thought for a moment before replying. *Well, my brotherly duty would be to accept you.*

I paused for a moment, looking at the brother I thought looked like me. I contemplated what he said and wondered why it was beginning to make sense. *Well, I'll be damned if I think of you as a Christian before I think of you as my own brother. You've been my brother for much longer, and I want to have that brother back.* I said this as I left his car and drove myself back to my apartment.

I would later convince myself that my brother's reaction was the result of years of constant comparison that came from the outside world, or that he was being protective of his own heterosexual identity. But maybe what he really felt was pity, and my newly claimed presence both offended and disgusted him in ways he was not prepared for.

Or that finally, I was a person he could never be.

Whatever it was for him, for me it was doubly painful. What hurt me more than anything else was the feeling that I no longer had a twin. The lack of symmetry in my life, at times harsh and cruel, at times beautiful and full of imperfection, was now taken away. My whole life had been spent trying to separate myself from my twin brother, and then when it happened, when the separation finally occurred more concretely than it had ever done so before, I was too scared to face the consequences.

The pain ran so deep not even Daniel could console me when I returned home in defeat. It was no longer liberating to know that I could finally exhale without inhaling another person's breath.

For two years I would love Daniel with a love my

brother would never know. It was difficult to not speak to Bobby at first. At times I found myself picking up the phone and dialing his number, only to hang up before he picked up the phone. Over time learning to not share my life with him became easier—so easy, in fact, that when the love I shared with Daniel finally took on a life of its own and outgrew the two of us, on that day when it became clear that neither he nor I could complete the other, it did not even occur to me to tell my brother about it. Even though I stayed awake endless nights while therapist after therapist likened my grief to the loss one feels when going through a divorce (how could it be divorce if our relationship was never validated?), I never once thought of sharing my pain with my twin brother.

And that was a sadness I was not prepared for.

35.

Bobby asked that I write him a letter. He asked that I write him as if writing him were the opposite of erasing him. As if writing him were a way of ensuring that even at that fateful hour when the study rejoined all that had been torn asunder, I would think of him even as I faced the tiring and uncertain day.

He asked that I write him, as if writing him would remind me of the promises we had made to each other and had since broken. As if all the conversations we had had over the years would somehow once again bind me to him. But my thoughts were chafed like wrists in metal shackles.

Still, I wrote:

> One boy sits atop the other—an other that looks just like him—and ties his hands above his head with an old shoe lace. "I'm not afraid, but what if something happens to you while I'm here, tied up like this? What happens if your heart were to simply stop?" His brother asks.
>
> The boy, continuing the knot, replies, "Everything, even your future, belongs to me."

This is the way boys grew up as twins in Providence, Rhode Island, in the 1970s. Ever since I tumbled out of the womb after my brother, I've learned what it means to follow. But I wrote more, since this is what he asked:

> I am balanced, juggling my life like a trapeze artist on some frayed wire counting how long it till take for my eyes to reach the ground, for the wind to automatically shift

direction and throw me somewhere on Route 128, for the
buzzing in my veins and the ringing in my loins like an
unanswered telephone to suddenly stop. And breathe in.
Breathe out. But as soon as I sit someone else stands. We
will never sit together; we don't know how. Even you. I
could once read your face like a children's book, but now
you're just letters fumbled in a cryptic anagram before me,
staring at me like owl's eyes. I love you, my enigma, my
foreign language, my darkened cave. Though you throw
me off balance in this high wire act. Earlier, there may
have been an extra bar to hold or a safety net below us,
but the circus has been taken down and folded away like
a Christmas quilt. And I am left on this wire, higher than
any pain or joy I could have found alone, wondering who
will catch me should I fall. . . .

And who will catch me? I thought, *Will it be God, with His hands always
outstretched? Will it be my brother, if for no other reason but for our shared
history?*

*Or will it be this virus, which I have come to embrace as
lover?*

Perhaps I should have paid more attention after
all, riding my bicycle along different routes so that I
would not have learned to love that which is forbidden. Instead of accepting love as a challenge to my
senses, I would see it as a form of comfort.

A lantern in winter.

A pillow for my head.

Instead I find beauty in its mystery until I am
forced to embrace my beloved like an addict embraces
a bottle, and I drink him ever so smoothly while the
clock continues to tick. It is then when I feel forced
to embrace my virus, love it like a sick, wounded friend
and nurse it back to health so it loves me in return.

I am a lover who would eat glass for my beloved.

36.

In order to understand our relationship, it is important to understand that this virus chose *me* for its lover; it was not the other way around. My beloved gave me things I never before had, the greatest of which was a life completely separate from my brother.

This virus found me, like an artist finds his canvas, and he has been painting me ever since.

People ask if we are newly partnered. I could say no. I could say yes. I often say nothing at all because there is so much more truth in silence. But in reality he's been with me longer than any lover I've ever known. He's defined me in ways no one else ever dared. He's been my identity since our union, and he's been an odd source of inspiration, a reason to get through the day, knowing, in some strange way, that in the evening, every evening, we would sleep together embraced in each other's arms. Such is the way with lovers.

And as his lover I want to write him anew because all that's been written about him has been written with images of war. I, myself, have been guilty of this infraction. Take the journal entry I wrote him on our second anniversary. Even its title sets the landscape for combat. I wrote:

> *Soldier: A Battle Hymn.* There is no scar at which we can look back and say heroically like a Persian Gulf soldier, *Remember the War of 1991?*

But we remember. We've seen the lesions line up at attention one by one, shoulder to shoulder. Scattered, shooting in open field, calling out melodious as taps *sound off one two sound off three four.* . . . We've heard the sound of our scabs dressed in army-issue green as they rip open like a troop of thieves & take away our beautiful skin, & spill on us like tear gas their drops of spoiled righteousness. . . . We've lost our sight for the memory of a stock & barrel lay. Triggers in our mouths, bullets in our blood. Now unable to recognize eyes & smiles. Seeing instead something shadowy shining like medals of honor. *All our lovers have gone AWOL,* the poet writes. All our lives discharged. . . . This is our war. Void of yellow ribbons & dollar-a-month veterans' life insurance policies. Old Glory now a term we use for life before the war. Back when we were brave & bronzed. When the ¼-inch cut of our hair told us we'd live to serve our country no matter what. . . .

Most wouldn't understand that my beloved and I are inseparable. But I'm sure my brother could because like the twinship he and I share, ours is a relationship born of mutual survival.

So it is no wonder that my beloved is only referenced in images of combat, because so many have gone on battling him, when all the while he was only asking to be embraced.

I've emerged from the ashes of a battle lost. I've emerged with all my energy drained from me like a syringe.

In retrospect my life was a series of actions leading up to this virus lover, and the moment he appeared everything around me started to make sense. This is how serendipity works. There is no real beginning, just an empty and lonely void hidden behind the surrounding ether. A world parallel only unto itself. A cloud that lifts itself over here. An incoherent voice falling over there. This was the world in which I lived.

And at the time my world was a geometry of sorts, a one-dimensional sideshow of lines and angles slapped upon circles without any sense of theorem or hypothesis. There was nothing to prove. No given facts to start off with. In this world I found myself torn, wandering the world at night under a sky that smelled of salt and a moon that found herself in Taurus. In this world the only movement was the wind as it moved among fields of grain. Wing of bird, static gold, and such and such. There I was, a timeless and amorphous thing, made of salt air and ocean tide. I had not yet taken form, yet he tried to sculpt me into whatever he wanted me to be. But he could not.

He wanted songs.

I wanted silence.

He said, *Give me what I want.*

I gave him songs with no words.

He tried to shape me, but the moon was already seated in her house, and the ocean rumbled on, both giving and taking life.

This is the beginning of our story. It is a story I am resigned to tell only in metaphor because the very nature of our relationship is abstract and non-linear and requires similar language to describe it.

Suffice it to say my problem was I always found the man in the moon. That vampire lover with folded wing who would turn to dust at sunrise. And each night was the same, only the faces changed. And every man I ever loved carried history between his legs like a lantern. Swinging with the heat of a thousand nights. In wintry caves, where ice refused to melt.

His Portuguese name was Paulo, and he was the kind of person who walked into a space and filled that space completely. And with him there was a time I would have pounced. There was a time I would have pounced on him like hunter on prey. Pounced in our jungle, tiger claw gripping monkey heart. Instead I studied him with a hungry eye. Studied him with a hungry eye as he poured forth with his words.

They came slowly at first, the game not suspecting the hunt. Slowly as in stroll. As in sauntering aimlessly. Slowly as in that something between a gallop and a trot.

I like the way your mind works, he said while I was still listening. *I like the way your mind works*, he said, and then something else. And then nothing else. That is, nothing else I could comprehend. His lips moved. His lips moved as though they were telling a story but the only sound I heard was the sound of the light as it hit his teeth. The sound of the light as it hit his teeth and the sound of his tongue pressing against his lips whenever he said the word *the*. Whenever he said the word *the* I witnessed the act of tongue against tooth against lip, and I felt thankful for just a moment for the frequency with which that little word repeats itself in the English language. *The. The. The.*

I knew then he had me completely under his control, never once thinking of the lesson I learned so many years ago as a child: that there is danger in trusting someone too quickly, and there is danger in giving your entire self for the feeling of warmth and comfort.

It could have been the gentle caress of his rough calloused hands upon my lips, half his age. Or it could have been the raging power of his kiss that seemed to feel its way inside me. Or perhaps it was the humility in his eyes as he bowed his head to smile. But there was something electric about him, about his fingertips, as they explored the hidden secrets of my skin.

And so he presented himself to me in the form of a lover. I did not hear the things he did not say, and instead heard the sound of the walls as they cracked around me. Never was it violent; instead, he welcomed me the way a lion welcomes the lamb when no one else is looking.

When all was done I stumbled to the font.

When all was done he said, *That was sweet. You were perfect.*

When all was said and done I wanted to be sweet and perfect.

And so, in an odd way, he was a type of Messiah. In him was the light of God shining like a stone in water. A voice running fingers through my hair. That day when he came into my life was summer and summer never felt so much like fall. The colors of the sky twisted themselves into grays and dark greens. The heat of the sun penetrated my skin like an early frost. Sound of birds leaving, rhythms of the street dying down to a torpid tempo. Was he man? Was he monster? Was he Messiah come to remind me that this is the kingdom, and the kingdom come? He was none of these things. He was all of these things.

The day this virus walked into my life—this man/monster/Messiah—he came to set me free. That day was like a page from an unfinished novel, as if the story I was reading suddenly unraveled itself like a thread and shed its words off the page. Each torn and fragmented letter lying on the floor without reason in an unsullied pile of ink. *There is something about you,* is what he said. *Something within you that both calms me and calls my name. It is calming and calling still.* Since that day, in me, he found respite. For him I wrote all sorts of songs. For him I wrote poems I wrote for none other:

Dirge for an Entertaining Host

I
i welcome you,
nameless, bouncing from cell to cell
a prisoner who never learns how to die
only how to kill

II
hiding behind liquid and bone,
just enough to make yourself known

III
and whoever used the term undetectable
studied a different kind of math than you did
you, whose numbers multiply daily, you
you you you you you
my exponential you

IV
i try to imagine what you are like
what personality you have hidden behind
those vacant eyes
what it is like to love someone so small
yet so large at the same time
and i watch you as you swing
back and forth in my head

like a palindrome,
sometimes melodic like Sexton
rats live on no evil star
other times haunting like a repeating burrow in my veins
and DNA and DNA and DNA

> V
> science tells the reader there are no words before it
> faith tells science that there are
> we read, regardless, with words in mind
> because, even invisible, you breathe

VI
you and i
we, two, became one
and the poet asked,
When did that happen?

VII
you have lived with me for a third
of my life, more than family, more
than friends, more than lovers
will you ever tire of my ways?

VIII
That I should embrace you is, perhaps, the
solution. That I should bring you home to
mother for Thanksgiving and Christmas and
proudly wrap my arms around you and say *This
is the one with whom I plan to spend the rest of
my life, this is the one with whom I will go to
the depths of hell, this is he, my new family,
who needs me in order to live.*

I wrote this because in many ways I felt the host
that sheltered him from the dangers of the outside

world: air, perhaps; alcohol for sure. And as his host I fed him morsels of my flesh and blood. And he, my parasite, took what he needed to survive.

What came next felt like a nuclear holocaust. The world inside me exploded. My head, some planetary mushroom. My eyes two innocent victims, witnesses to the radioactive toxin in my body. I became an atom, split. The blue floated to my skin and opened like an eye watching the world watch it. Like a blue walnut carrying the weight of his words like a dark and heavy stone.

Blue to purple to black to blue to yellow.

To nothing.

All in a matter of days: a bloom at first.

A thick and heavy vine.

To trickle . . . to nothing.

I was only I trying to save you, is what I said.

The virus was the beloved who eventually found me, not the man who harbored it. The man who harbored it was much more afraid of the world, afraid to let himself be known for fear that his wife and child might discover any one of his many secrets. And so I released him to the night. After several months of him loving the way my mind works, I released him, until all that was left were the coffee grounds that connected evening to morning, and the cigarette lighter that saved him when he ran out of his supply of words and left the conversation dangling like a broken arm. I recall his face, noting for months how it glowed like a birthday cake when he lit his cigarette, which he cupped in the palm of his hand to protect the flame from spilling into the wind of my words. Words he chose not to hear true and sharp, unstained like a new razor, leaving me erased and lost in monologue.

When he left I began my inward retreat to that

place where I curled up inside myself like a leaf on fire, to the land of coho salmon and eagles, where I was endangered even unto myself, leaning on the edge of extinction.

I have only these memories to hold on to: the names he called me and no one else; the stories we told in the middle of the night; the summer skies that parted to let in the moon.

And so is the story of how my beloved sought me out, the story I never publicly disclosed. I am convinced I loved the man through whom he appeared. I loved that man with a depth I never knew I could feel, and in the brief months we spent together, I welcomed the virus within me. A strange product of the both of us.

And in doing so, I reached the point in my own growth where I was completely and unequivocally distinguishable from my brother. My union with this virus would come to represent the epitome of my life with a new and different twin. He would be my new identity, my new doppelgänger, my universe in which my brother can only be spectator.

It's an identity I can either choose to embrace, or one that will haunt me all the days of my life.

Considering the framework of our lives, there is solace in saying it's part of what makes me unique. For this reason alone, I embrace him.

But embracing him is not enough to satisfy my need to be. I must love him and care for him and nurture him the way lovers nurture and care for one another. After all, this is the one with whom I will spend the rest of my life.

And whether I planned it this way or not, if there is one thing I've learned in being an identical twin, it's that each person has the right to be bound to another.

Why should this be any different with my beloved?

37.

After two months I felt the first symptoms. It started with a cough that lingered like a hot dagger in my throat. A few days later I went to see my doctor who convinced me to take an HIV test. *The results will take about two weeks*, he said. He then told me I should feel good that this is not pneumonia, but I could not even smile without my face feeling the rip. Two days later the fevers came, and then the early morning sweats that left me prostrate in my bed like a crucifix. I knew then that I had it, but I did not want to admit it.

The call came on my twenty-fifth birthday. *I'm sorry to tell you this, but the test came back positive.* My doctor went on to say something about false positives and then something about something else. I stopped listening.

For three days I did not sleep a wink. I was like the princess and the pea, only instead of a princess I was a prisoner faced with a lifetime sentence, and the pea of my diagnosis was a hard, pointy boulder. The first person I told was Daniel. He spent the night with me and rocked me to sleep, a surrogate mother to the orphan that had formed inside me. It was the first time I had slept since receiving the news, and each tired, infected cell in my body fell into that sleep and welcomed it like a long-lost friend.

How do I tell my family? I asked the next morning.

Do you have to? Was his reply.

Oh, yes! I said without thinking first. It was clear to me that I did not have to tell anyone, at least not until I was ready, but at the same time there was no doubt that I needed my brother with me more than I ever needed him in my entire life.

38.

I learned it all from first grade to fifth when I learned the components of a sentence, when I learned that the beauty of language is that we are all part of that language, that as we study what it means to be a noun, or a verb, or an adjective we also, simultaneously, as if the universes of emotion and alphabet were suddenly fused into one, *feel* what it means to be a noun, or a verb, or an adjective, and at that moment of fusion, when life becomes the word on paper, I finally come to terms with my life: a sentence, a line of words strung together sometimes with meaning, sometimes without meaning, always containing those things a sentence always seems to contain, like a noun, a common noun at that, like *faggot* (as in *God hates a faggot*, but not as in *God hates your faggot ways* because then I am no longer a noun, but an adjective, and that, you will find, comes much later in life), so instead my life, at this moment, is a noun—sometimes a common noun but then sometimes a proper noun (as in *Tommy*), or a compound noun (as in *twinship*), or a collective noun (as in *the genes that made us this way*), or a possessive noun (as in *I am and I will always be, my brother's keeper*); and only once I am a noun, whether it be a common noun or a proper noun or a collective noun or a possessive noun—something inside me yearns to be, something inside yearns to give the nouns in my life meaning, and it is only when the desire to be burns inside like an ember struggling to stay lit do I suddenly unfold and become a verb—an inactive verb today (to be, as in *I am gay*), an active verb tomorrow, as in *replicate* (like carbon copies, or identical twins, or infectious viral particles); and as a verb I will be a variety of tenses, sometimes more than one simultaneously, sometimes just present (*I have AIDS*), sometimes present continuous (*I am trying to tell you I have AIDS*), sometimes just past (*I tried to tell you I have AIDS*), and sometimes future (*I will die with this disease*); regardless of which, I can be one or I can be all, but I will always be tense, and once I've seen myself as noun and verb I will slowly grow into adjective to describe myself and make myself more interesting to you, my audience, so that you will no longer see me as *your twin* but instead will come to know me as *your gay HIV-positive twin*, and to the parents who once knew me as *their son* I will be remembered as *their sick son*, sick from too much language and too much love, adjectives can do that to a person, and sometimes the adjective I become is multiple in meaning, and so I am split (as in *zygote*) and split (as in *personality*)—the adjectives I become can be confusing to a person; the adverb, on the other hand, disassociates itself from the subject and marries itself instead to its action; so, whereas I love, I can now love too *deeply*, and whereas I cry, I now cry *passionately*, and when it comes to loving, and when it comes to crying the sentence of my life takes on objects, and when those objects are direct I no longer love too deeply, instead I love *you* too deeply, and when those objects are indirect I no longer cry passionately, I cry passionately only *for you*, and so it is, as is the case with most twins, that the components of my life take on meaning and structure, and my life becomes the very sentence I use to describe it; yet like a sentence, as in the string of words full of subject and predicate, my life, too, is another sentence, a prison sentence, as in removed from the outside world, a sentence as in a final verdict, a judgment, a lack of freedom, or a loss of freedom once owned, a life once held in the palm of my hand and then taken away, forever, leaving me with only a series of words never without a verb to follow; otherwise, if I could, I'd be *individual* or *asexual* or *undetectable*: words all by themselves.

39.

Bobby? I asked when he picked up the phone. And without missing a beat, my Corsican twin immediately felt my distress.

What happened? He asked. *What's wrong?*

Bobby, I need to talk to you, and I need to talk to you now. It's important. We met at a nearby park and it was there, with the sun reaching the end of its day, that I shared the news with him. *My doctor told me this week that I have HIV.* I said it with a crack in my voice, completely unable to look him in the face. I was ready for his judgment; I was ready for his scorn. I was prepared to walk through those if that's what it took to get my brother back. I remember the heat of the day, and I remember the sun's last glimmer of light as we behaved as though the distance between us never existed.

But there was no judgment. No scorn. Instead my brother took my hand and insisted that I get tested again, deciding to go with me when the test results were ready. He acted as though this thing had infected us both. After all, twins are supposed to be inseparable. But who decides what that means? Do we choose those moments of togetherness and separation? Does fate somehow twist itself with twins in ways it cannot with others? Were we really just two halves of a larger whole?

So there we found ourselves in June 1990, Bobby in his denial, and I in my shame. We waited, sitting in two chairs in a cold and concrete room facing a cinder block wall where the temperature reached eighty degrees, and a door with a sign that read, *Rhode Island Department of Health. PRIVATE.* In my hands I held a sheet of paper that identified me as "2874-M" and nothing else. My foot tapped on the floor with no attempt to be subtle as Bobby and I awaited my test results.

Positive. The social worker repeated the word slowly, as if examining it for flaws before releasing it. *Positive.*

Everything else sped past me as if I were fast forwarding through a horror movie. I remember hearing something like, *Rhode Island Project AIDS*, and, *Insurance coverage*, and, *You don't want to make any drastic changes right now in your life, like quitting your job or going back to school. Let it sink in.*

And I wanted it all to be a lie, for my brother and I to once again become one. We had grown too far apart. I felt a fear that left me frozen with the knowledge that one of us was being banished to a world the other knew nothing about. All I wanted was for us to return to that place of cadence and symmetry, where life could not touch one of us if it could not touch us both.

I tried to listen to what the social worker had to say, but her sentences seemed to struggle with themselves. The drone of her words became muffled and muted as I tried not to notice that this moment, separated from all other moments in time, would now define us forever.

I would be the *positive* one. My brother would be the *negative*.

How would that feel? Would we be like two ionic charges of a battery, each needing the other in order to function fully? Or would we finally be independent of the other?

This was the first time we had to face our own mortality. We were twenty-five years old and both of us, in one way or another, found ourselves living with a death sentence. Mine a literal one, his something more vicarious. I thought about what it would mean for me to die before seeing thirty, but the hardest part was thinking what all this would mean for my brother.

What happens to the surviving twin when his brother dies? Does he mourn the death of his brother as well as that part of him his brother has taken to the grave, their identities in some ways inseparable? Does the solitude that follows affect him the same way it affects a singleton who has lost a sibling, or is everything doubled in intensity?

And of course, the biggest question of all: When all is said and done, would the survivor still be a twin?

40.

What would it have been like if one of the doctors dressed in green scrubs from head to toe and a white overcoat had come running into my room, arms flailing as wildly as his stethoscope, and announced, *My God, it worked! It really worked! There is no trace of HIV in your system at all . . . ?*

What if the treatment proved successful, and instead of reminding myself that yes, the official diagnosis is—and will always be—AIDS, I would convince myself that my body is once again brand new?

What if it had been like the time I was diagnosed with liver damage, and I sat in the bathtub and listened to a cassette tape of water trickling down a brook and imagined myself pouring a magical elixir over my sick gray organ, cradling it in my arms the way a mother cradles a baby, all the while washing it until it once again became a healthy pink, and doctors proclaimed, *It's a miracle, that power of visualization!* What if this time had been like that?

I'm not sure how I would have reacted, but I don't think it would have been a happy thing. Instead, I suspect it would have been like a beautiful room that had just been emptied of all its fine furnishings. A luxurious carpet lifted or a sculpture of the living suddenly dissolved. All the things that made the room would forever be gone.

There would have been a mourning of sorts, having

lived my life betrothed to my beloved only to find he was now undetectable.

There would have been a mourning indeed.

I suspect I would have had to learn to live again, a form of rehabilitation for the dispossessed.

In less than twenty-four hours the experiment will have begun, I thought, *and I will finally be reminded why I am here in this hospital on the hill. What will that be like? Will we simultaneously feel the power of that moment like a cataclysm? Or will it simply wash through us like saline through open veins?*

There were too many thoughts and too many memories racing through my mind all at once. In the course of a single evening my entire life was a movie reel playing itself over and over and over again in my mind.

This is the way my memory works: I am shown something and I look at it for a moment. I contemplate its purpose in my life. I imagine life without it. If I can live without it, I will forget it. If I cannot, it will stay with me forever.

I hold on to all my memories of my twin brother because they are the only things keeping me alive.

And this is how I measure my love for someone else: I ask myself how I would feel the day he dies. Though not a popular strategy, it allows me the pleasure of releasing myself from such wearying factors as whether or not we belong to the same family. If I smile a faint, hidden smile and whisper, *At least he is no longer suffering,* then I never loved him, because only a fool would take solace in such a sacred act as death. And if I were to say nothing, reminding myself that death is a part of life, leaves fall, seasons change, and such and such, then I loved him the way a child loves the summer, carrying the memory with him each year long past his prime. But if I were to curse the sky, to want to soar toward God, clenched fists before me, spit in my mouth, splitting the sky in two with the vengeance of a war plane, stopping only when I feel the shell of God crack in my bleeding hands, only then will I know that I loved him with a love that forever leans and never falls. A solid love. A stone.

This is how I love my brother.

So I knew I must, too, come to love this body. Let us not underestimate its power. I carried myself to the bathroom and undressed before the mirror. It was not a full-length mirror, but fairly large, and tilted toward the ground so that a person in a wheelchair could still use it. As I stood and studied myself, I stood and studied my twin brother.

I knew I must, too, come to love this body because naked, from head to toe, we two were one.

The body is not a perfect thing, but it remembers. It remembered the time my brother and I were both sick with pertussis, him beside me crying between coughs and pleading, *Pray for me, Tommy. Please pray for me*, as I rubbed his back in a circular motion. And it remembered when we as children used to catch flies with our bare hands. We would feel their wings pitter-patter as they tried to escape the wall of our fists, shaking like a rattlesnake as we tossed them onto the deadly pavement that awaited their death without warning.

What I want to tell you, Bobby, I thought, *is that today I am that fly. I am the one whose world closes in like a fist, blocking out the light from my vision. In a matter of time I will be weak and dizzy from the ride and the rattle. My wings will fold themselves across me and tuck me away like a letter in an envelope. They will cease to work and will leave me in the cracks in the pavement with the others who have tried to escape, only this time being warned.*

And, of course, the body knew that now I was the one asking you for a prayer before a mirror in an experimental hospital, and that I had somehow become that fly—the one whose world closes in like a fist, blocking out the light from my vision. In its slight imperfection the body knew that in a matter of time I would be weak and dizzy from the ride and the rattle.

41.

His name was Jim, and with him I learned that being in grief is nothing like being in love, despite the same unbridled passion. The same need to merge two bodies into one.

I loved him with the innocence of youth, but my youth is what made him afraid to love me back. I was too young, twenty years his junior, to be exact. In his eyes, I was a child who could not understand love. In my eyes, we made each other laugh and we made each other cry, and such talents have no age requirements.

Instead, he sealed himself like a letter, hiding from me the secret I would eventually come to find out, trying to convince us both, unsuccessfully, *Really, could this ever work out?*

I remember cutting my finger on a knife in my kitchen before going out for dinner. *You wouldn't want to watch a man try to eat dinner with a bandaged finger,* I said, creating conversation as I wrapped the bandage around my finger.

I'll feed you if I have to. This is what love is supposed to be about.

His death was the more painful because for six months prior he locked himself inside his house and prevented anyone from visiting. Phone calls were never returned. Mail left unanswered. I wanted contact with the universe that was now his; he wanted to disconnect me from it entirely. Perhaps he thought it a type of protection to not see him that way, and I tried to tell myself that, knowing all the while the reality remained: I was disconnected from his world the way electricity is disconnected after an electrical storm.

And with us, the lights never came back on. The conversations ceased to take place, but if I could, I'd start them again.

Conversation with Jim on a Hill

not a hill more like a mound a plot of dead
land a patch of dirt & newly planted grass
laid out in this cemetery which spreads itself
like a quilt here on this patch just one week
before Memorial Day no not a week nine
days to be exact May 19 2001 here I sit on
this patch of dirt & newly planted grass
something sacred now because of you
something which calls me back from
Minnesota back two thousand miles to the
Notre Dame Cemetery 1540 Stafford Road
Fall River Massachusetts Lot 73 Section 2
to a tombstone marked Viveiros your
mother's maiden name—who was it that
once told me that we Portuguese are really
immortal that death is just a phase we go
through—how I wish I could believe that
now how I wish I could believe that here on
this same plot of dirt & grass I visited nine
years ago

There are flowers here for you flowers by
your plot many flowers tell me someone else
has visited you recently it was someone else
not I who left these flowers you see today

instead I hold a pamphlet of the *Rules &*
Regulations of the cemetery rules &
regulations that say all flowers placed at
grave sites become the property of the
cemetery & will be used to beautify the
grounds & I think to myself were you not
enough to make this somber place more
beautiful were you not enough that they
need to take your flowers too I've given
them enough they do not need the flowers
you dear Jim were enough I've given them
you but who was it who visited you last who
else could never forget the meal you fed me
at that restaurant on Thayer Street when my
thumb was sliced & sutured & bandaged so
that I could not even lift my fork or the way
your shoulders moved up & down like a man
on a string whenever you laughed or the
beauty mark on your right cheek which
charmed the world like a newborn
babe or your eyes two chestnuts always
looking up or up to something was I not
enough for you Jim who else but I visited
your classroom pretending to take notes on
the science of instruction instead writing
love poems which would never be read
aloud & who but I Jim shivered when you
winked as your students called you Mr.
Costa who else Jim who else visited you
when you shriveled away & who asked why
do you watch the home shopping club so
much & you replied it's the only company I
have these days & now even now who else
but I stretch themselves upon this patch of
land your little plot of earth & offer
themselves to you just six feet above nine

years later at this cemetery plot two
thousand miles away & whisper prostrate
arms stretched in crucifixion *Jim, dear Jim,
you left this world too soon!*

At this moment I want the world to stop
turn my gaze to the wind which blows east
toward the ocean cresting somewhere off
these shores I want to stop time for just a
few moments I want to but never could stop
time instead the ocean is cresting still the
same way it did on July 28 1992 at 17
Brigham Street in Rumford Rhode Island the
ocean is cresting still as if the shores have
suddenly forgotten what to do Jim, I cannot
stop this crest.

It's one thing to watch those you love slowly die
before your eyes, but it's another thing altogether
when you know that what is killing them is exactly
what is killing you. I tried to be strong for Jim, reminding him of all the scientific progress that had
been made in the previous year. Believing whole-
heartedly that if there were anyone who would survive this thing it would surely be him. And then,
when I went home at the end of the day, I went to
sleep at night, holding myself as if I were coming
apart at the seams, afraid that my own stuffing might
leak out at any time.

42.

There were nights I wanted to call him. There were the nights I needed to hear my brother's voice to remind me that neither of us was leaving soon. That despite the teachings of the church I had come to reject, he was still praying for me, daily, and waiting for God just like I was.

I could not make this thing any uglier than it already was. Yet in my quest to find myself I had somehow failed the both of us, and there was now no turning back. I had gone to that extreme place where I finally succumbed to the world around me and opened myself to society's probe to become a thing vivisected, in its atom state.

I became microscopic in my own illness.

My deepest regret was letting it pull me further and further away from my brother. Our bond was no match for the church, and in the end I left it. I had to. For two years all our conversations ended in Bible verse battles, and it was easier for me to keep silent instead of attempting to bridge the gap that had so widely opened between us.

My priorities shifted to learning how to survive.

We were distant, yet I knew I needed him in my life. But how would that happen? Would I pick up the phone one day out of spontaneity and speak as if nothing had happened, knowing all along that it is exactly because of this silence that countless others living with this disease are allowed to die all around us? Do I raise the issues cautiously, one by one, holding them up like flowers in a bouquet repeating only to myself, *He loves me, he loves me not; he loves me, he loves me not?*

I was afraid to speak to my brother because every time I tried to do so the conversation always turned into a theological battle. I wonder if he ever noticed how those Bible verses separated us and never even tried to reunite us.

I came to hate the Book of Romans.

In reality, if I could have, I would have told my brother that I was a shepherd leading a blind flock behind me across this barren land we think will somehow spring forth life as if by magic or some holy dove. And that I was an eye bleeding, reacting only to blurs in my vision, and keeping my distance from all those lines and figures that scare me away. My brother's Bible was like that. Its title was simple, a nursery rhyme full of all the things that folktales are made of, but the power of its words—those long short curves and lines that only those not blind can read—can transform man into beast to practice hatred as if it were the Spirit's tenth fruit.

But my journey was not so manipulative. I was simply walking, looking for life once again and for the man I knew as Jesus.

If I could, I would have told my brother that Jesus was, perhaps, the tablet I pounded daily into powder that, when mixed with water, fooled my immune system into believing it was alive. That dust that kept me going back for more like communion wafers from dirty hands. Or perhaps he was the sound of the waves as they threw themselves into the cliffs in a sweet meditative visual; or the man lying next to me who rocked me to sleep on those nights that found me lying with one eye open, waiting, alert, for my killer.

This was the gospel according to John Thomas. This was the gospel we'd never read. The good news we had yet to be told. And all the while we rose, arms hanging on us like bags of sand. We rose, if not from our beds at least from our sins. We rose.

And the resurrection came sweetly.

Such were the thoughts that came to me during the Lenten season, a time of reflection on the last steps of Christ, of Christ's death, and, ultimately, his Resurrection. I believed God was diverse, with diverse ways of worshiping Him. I believed God showed Himself to us in a myriad of ways, varying from person to person.

I believed, simply, that the tools God put in my life to experience His being were not the same as those put in my brother's life, and neither way was more or less valid than the other.

Did it need to be any more complicated than that?

43.

Two years. That's how much time had to pass for my brother and I to speak to each other once again. And during that time we maintained a silence and a distance neither of us really wanted. Perhaps it was his church that kept us apart, but deep inside I knew it was also my shame. I had failed the ultimate test, and in doing so created a future for us both that neither of us wanted. I wrote him a letter that I knew I would never send.

Dear Bobby,

I'm sorry I've not been in contact for quite some time. I've been learning to adjust to this new death-sentence reality. Some days I find myself spinning in circles, knowing my days are numbered, other days I can't look in the mirror. My doctor says I won't make it to thirty. Such statistics are not consoling. I want you to be a part of my world again. I want us to laugh like we used to and be there for each other. But you have your life, and I have mine.

And what is it like, this personal pandemic? It starts with fear, a fear that is both consuming and elusive. I'm not afraid of feelings; they just hang on me like oversized suits, cadaver-black and napkin-starched. For the first time in my life, I find myself afraid of words. They stalk me, make me a blueprint and reveal all my closets and secret hideaways. Words have the power to become real.

For example, I must say I am ready for this virus. Ready to waken one minute past midnight, limp and wet like a cold fish in a sea of bedsheet, watching, waiting for the herons to fly low. I'm ready for the bumblebees to move marching-band slow in my veins, the same march over and over and over again in their brass cacophony. Ready for my sky to crack open with a thousand and one violins. For solitaire to go into overtime. For time to shine upon me like a sundial, my shadow slowly getting smaller and smaller in the west-setting sun. I am ready for my hungry words to swallow me like an epitaph, turn themselves into numbers.

I am ready to start counting backward because it has come to this: Me, twenty-seven years old, against a virus almost two. A Tarot card that shows me my day's end like an old woman caressing her crystal ball. An injection that taints my body and leaks from me like a syringe. I cling to a number, five-hundred and forty. This is the highest my cells will ever be, counting down to their own Armageddon.

After fear comes the endless waiting for things to get back to normal. I find myself learning that this is how you look at life from death at twenty-seven, when time sheds its immortality like a leper through all its dog-eared pages: you watch the helper cells join the invaders, the numbers start high and slowly—no, not slowly, quickly—plummet into Armageddon and leave you all alone. That is your new lot in life. And while your love is both weapon and shield, it is not enough to win this battle.

Bobby, what I want to say is that life at this moment seems so quantifiable. I can weigh it like dead meat and by the medications I am forced to take. When I run out of them or when they no longer work (there still is no cure), I'll know my time is up. Only then will I be left with just memories of life before this war.

I would love to sit at home on weekday afternoons, you and I racing to be the first to turn on the TV to do nothing more than watch cartoons and eat Kellogg's Corn Flakes with extra sugar, counting time by the TV commercials. But instead I must go for my weekly injection of Procysteine, running up the stairs to make it easier for the nurse to find a good vein, now telling time by the five-minute infusions.

This is my first experimental treatment (other than those chocolate bars made with fish oil, which I'd rather not get into). My home right now is the Day Treatment Center on the fourth floor, east wing left. This place is strange somehow. People leave and enter like shoppers in a mall. Such a short-term place for a long-term illness.

There are nurses, three, whose job it is to smile as they hook the old man up to a chemo IV as if it were a band-aid on a scraped knee. They are like this all the while as they take temperature and blood from me to prepare for the experiment: a drug handmade like an old woman's secret recipe.

I am on my way. The liquid pushes itself inside me like a wet, cold finger from an old man's hand. The voices in my head still linger, haunting like a shadow in a strange land. I pray. I have seen schools turn into hospitals over-night. I've witnessed the death of Bugs Bunny, slow to come like Christmas to a child. And I've watched in fear as the television, as if by magic, transformed itself into IV tubes. As a boy, still, I have seen it all.

And throughout at it all you are there, my hero, by my side.

I will wait for you to arrive.

Your twin,
Tommy

I wrote several letters like that during those two years. That was when I moved to Boston, where I lived with a partner who always played sec-ond fiddle to this virus.

While I lived with him I committed adultery. I cheated on him with the hope of a cure. The thought of disrobing myself of all this useless flesh, molting like a young snake. My smile wide like a slice of sky,

my eyes the sun and the moon turned on like opening night on Broadway. If good health were my neighbor and a cure his wife then I had broken the Tenth
Commandment, flirted with the thought of clothing
myself with an endless string of pearls still warm
from their oyster bellies.

And all this is metaphor. The virus inside me
reminded me that it is primary to any man I could
ever love. For two years I lived this way in Boston: I
simultaneously craved and cringed at the thought of
another man. The clock on the mantel reminded me
every fifteen minutes that my skin would turn to
leather before being touched. My house sealed me
like a tomb. This was my new unsustaining reality.

And when those two silent years passed, only then
did I hear from the National Institutes of Health. I was
wrapping up my work at the hospital where I coordi-
nated AIDS services in Somerville, Massachusetts,
having made the decision to move to Minnesota,
where friends there convinced me that I needed a
change to a place where the pace was a bit slower
and the healthcare a bit better.

The phone call took me by surprise.

This is Betty, from the NIH, said the voice on the other end. *We have not
forgotten you.* Ironic, because I had forgotten her.

She went on to say something about how the latest study they were
conducting was a gene therapy study for identical twins, and not a bone
marrow study. She went on to talk about how my brother and I had to
pay airfare and accommodations for the first visit to Bethesda, and how
we would have to undergo a series of tests to evidence that our *twinship*
was identical.

Twinship was the word she used. *Twinship* was a word I had never
heard before.

She mentioned something about meeting with case managers and
doctors to review protocols and sign consent forms. But all that kept
going through my mind was how I was going to tell my brother. I realized

at that moment that I never mentioned any of this to him, and that his consent was needed as much as mine, and we weren't even talking to each other. After so many years of learning to be independent of him, I found myself needing him once again. And I wondered if the past two years meant as little or as much to him as they did to me.

And so I sat in the confines of my office allowing myself to be wrapped up in thoughts of what would happen from this point on. This was the moment of impact, the moment when I could no longer deny that I needed to call my twin brother into the fold and openly admit that I needed him. I'd lived for so many years convincing myself that he was no longer required for me to be myself. In the end, it only took a government-funded identical twin gene therapy study to show me how critical my brother was to my survival.

I studied every item in my office, from the tall floor lamp that flickered its light, to the filing cabinet marked "HIV Advocacy Materials," to the Peruvian wall hanging that contained the figures of ten fish, each alternating in direction from east to west, right to left, as if to give the impression of a circular and unending motion. That wall hanging was a gift from a friend in college to remind me that Christ is always with me. And as I contemplated the gift and all its many meanings, its diversity, its colors, its strength, I practiced the conversation I would have with my brother for several days before I finally called.

Hello. Bobby's words were a statement more than a question, and his voice was rushed and gravelly when he picked up the phone, as if I caught him in the middle of the rinse cycle, or, more appropriately, his favorite pro basketball game.

It's me, Tommy, I said, not bracing myself for what I would follow this with. So I took the easy way out and opted with the ever safe, *You busy?*

No, no. Not at all. Just give me a second to close the door. I waited for the moments to pass by like hours. *What's up?*

I need to talk with you about something, I said. *Something serious, only I don't really know how to, so I'm just going to come right out with it.*

Okaaay. And although I couldn't see him, I could tell he was sitting himself down. This is how he braces himself for unexpected news.

I've been researching something I want to share with you. In fact, I've been hold-

ing off on telling you about it, but can't really hold off on it any longer. It's an experimental study for HIV treatment.

I'd come to learn over the years that many people, my brother included, respond better when those of us living with this disease refer to it as *HIV* and not *AIDS.*

I continued. *In fact, I've been on a waiting list for about two years now for this study, and I was recently called up.* I paused for a moment. *It's a study involving identical twins.* I somehow knew that would pique his interest.

Really? Identical twins? That sounds interesting.

Neither of us mentioned God. Neither of us acknowledged the silent distance of the past two years, save an awkward Christmas or two. This has always been the way with us; when we are called to act on the most visceral of levels nothing gets in the way of that.

Well, I don't really know all the details, but from what I know, they take your cells, do something to them so they are uninfectable, and then grow them in large numbers and then give them to me. It's called gene therapy, and since we have the same genetic makeup, the idea is that I'd be able to reproduce your uninfectable cells pretty easily. With each passing moment I could feel the anxiety pulse like an arhythmic heartbeat.

But you're in Boston, about to move to Minnesota, and I'm in Rhode Island. Where is this study going to take place? My brother asked.

It's still several months away before we'll actually start, but the study's being conducted by the National Institutes of Health in Bethesda, Maryland. You and I will each have to pay for our own airfare out there for the very first trip, but once we're accepted into the study they'll pay for everything else after that.

I see . . . accepted into the study, he repeated. *What's it take to get accepted into the study?*

Well, they'll need to test us to make sure that we are, in fact, identical twins.

You mean they're going to verify that we're identical?

Yes. We have to be in order to qualify for the study, so they have to test for that.

Wow. He paused for a moment to take in all the wonders a single moment can hold. *Can you imagine just for a second what it would be like if we were to find out, after living the past twenty-eight years of our lives as identical twins, that we really aren't identical? Wouldn't that just blow you away?*

And I paused for a moment, not saying a word, feeling a heavy stone in my stomach. Screw them all, I thought, knowing that regardless of what the tests showed, we are identical. Of course we are identical, without a doubt. But then the thought hit me: if we are truly identical, it would suggest we would each spend the exact same amount of time on this earth as the other. That logic would follow that, since my brother was born two minutes before I was, he would also die two minutes before I would. Right? But that can't possibly be true.

Perhaps I did not want our twinship to be identical, after all.

I went back to the topic at hand. *I'm not sure about you, but I'm pretty sure we're identical,* I said, half joking, half brushing aside the notion and moving on to more serious matters, like whether or not he was planning to participate in the study with me. *Well, anyway, the truth of the matter is this—I obviously cannot participate in this study without you.* I knew what I wanted to say, and knew that if I did not say it at that very moment, I would regret it for the rest of my life.

In other words, I really need this, and I really need you. I said it. I could not look up, but I said it and that's what mattered. *So, is this something you can do with me?*

There was a silence that was beyond uncomfortable. He knew it was hard for me to tell him that I need him, even though needing him was what my childhood was all about. I needed him to stand up for me to the bullies in our school. I needed him to fight for me when others picked on me, and to make the other students and sometimes, even teachers, laugh because laughing meant they liked him, which I took to mean they also liked me because, after all, we were inseparable. He knew I would not tell him now that I needed him unless I was absolutely desperate. His silence lingered ever longer, and I grew more anxious. It's not so much that it took him a long time to give me a response as much as it took all the eternities a single moment can hold to consider every possibility available to me in the event that he said no.

But instead, with the comforts and wisdom that take on an entirely different meaning when spoken by one twin to another, he simply said, *Of course. You should know by now that what's mine also belongs to you. . . .*

And for the first time in my adult life I felt proud of him, knowing I was a carbon copy of him.

The distance that grew between us the past two years was there only so we could appreciate the closeness that moment had brought us.

44.

Identity. Identical.

Is it coincidence that these words are so closely and properly related, as if to imply that what makes us identical is that which gives us our very identity? Perhaps this has been nature's design all along, that as twins, my brother and I would not have an identity separate from the other, and simply being identical was all we ever needed to be. If this is the case, then my search for identity has really been a search *out of* an identity I had not chosen. To think it took so long to learn that.

They say it's a myth that identical twins experience greater challenges in establishing their individual identities, but with my brother and me, it was true. Of course the fact that we resemble each other complicates the process of being whole. But individuality is much more complicated than that. If others see us as one unit, then we develop similarities in our identity, at times preventing ourselves from ever becoming individual and whole. And if we perceive our twin nature as the primary focus in our lives, then our identities become fused with each other.

These truths revealed themselves the time my brother helped me move to Minnesota. I had saved a little bit of money, but I was given funding from an organization that granted wishes to those living with HIV. My wish was a modest one—just enough funds to rent a truck that I could use to drive me and my belongings from Massachusetts to Minneapolis, where a new job and a new life awaited me. I knew I couldn't make the trek alone, and I knew the only person I wanted to join me was my brother. Being on a long journey with another person can be a nightmare if it's the wrong person, but I figured since Bobby and I had already been together on the long journey of our lives, he'd be the ideal road companion.

Got a minute? I asked when I caught him on the phone. *You know next week I'm driving to Minnesota.* I had already broken the news to the family. *I am going to rent a truck and drive there. I mean from Boston to Minneapolis.* I fumbled my words, looking for the right way to ask if he'd like to join me.

Bobby beat me to the finish line. *You can't do that alone, especially in January! Are you crazy? You should let me come with you. It'll be fun.* His offer to drive halfway across the country with me was one I held tightly.

Long road trips start out with the trivial conversations. How beautiful things are on the side of the road. Guesses about the habits of local townspeople. And then the conversations become more reflective. *I think it's awesome that we're going to be in this twin study together,* Bobby started. *I mean, think about it, no one else in our family can be in this study except you and me. That's pretty cool!* I like to think by "cool" he meant that it was something that would bring us even closer.

Better than cool, I said. *It's going to change our lives.*

And the trip remained pleasant for the next several hundred miles. I woke up at just past midnight in a town somewhere in western Pennsylvania. *What's up?* I asked.

We need to get gas, he said, pulling in to the exit lane.

There's a gas station just off the exit, I replied *Let's just go there so we can get back on the highway.*

The gas station was the only thing off the highway, other than a long unlit road that went endlessly north. And for a reason I could not understand, Bobby drove right past the gas station and continued north. *What are you doing?!* I shouted. *You just passed the gas station! Where the hell are you going?!*

Well, I thought I'd see if there was another gas station up the road where the gas might be a bit cheaper.

You thought?! Bobby, it's midnight, and there aren't even any streetlights on that road. While you were thinking, did you happen to think about how narrow this road is, or that with us driving this truck and my car in tow, we can't even turn around? Did you think about that? Actually, why don't you tell me what the fuck were you thinking! My anger was in full throttle. *You never listen to me!*

Okay, dammit! I just wanted to see what was ahead, Bobby said. *Why do you never let me make mistakes?! Nobody is allowed to make a mistake around you.*

We were now almost two miles from the gas station. Pissed off, my brother decided to turn the truck around in the middle of the road, pulling off in a ditch on the left-hand side of the road. But it was pure ice, so whereas we were able to turn the truck around, we were not able to get it out of the ditch. Every attempt we made only resulted in the truck sliding back down into the ditch.

Great! Fucking great! I yelled. *We're stuck on an unlit road in the middle of January in a town we don't even know and no way to get out. Tell me,* I said, *while you were thinking, did you think about how we can get out of this mess?!*

Without saying a word, Bobby began to walk to the gas station, mumbling something that sounded very much like *fuck off!* under his breath.

It took almost two hours for a tow truck to rescue us, and for us to fill the gas tank and get back on the highway.

That's two hours we'll never get back, I said. I was too tired to say more than that. And with that I fell asleep.

The next thing I knew the sun was out and we were at a truck stop in Indiana. Bobby stopped to get something to eat, and not knowing if we passed from Eastern time to Central time, he asked a local if he knew what time it was.

What time is it? The man asked. *What time is it? Boy, you on God's time!*

I told Bobby to get in the passenger's seat so that I would take over the driving and he happily obliged. *Let's get the hell out of here,* Bobby said, half-jokingly. *Did you hear that man say we're on God's time when I asked him what time it was? Shit, this place is scary.*

That's when we both laughed.

Another thing about long road trips is that when you argue, you are forced to reconcile; otherwise, the rest of the trip will be just plain miserable. With Bobby and me the reconciliation came easier than I thought it would.

When you told me you were gay, Bobby admitted, *I felt like you took something away from me.*

Well, when you told me it was your Christian obligation to tell me I'm going to hell, I felt I lost you forever. I felt you were asking me to accept you as a different person than the brother I had come to know and love.

At that moment it became clear to both of us that although others had stopped comparing us to each other years ago, we had never stopped comparing us to ourselves. As a result, we never allowed the other to grow completely. We had prevented the other from being who he is and instead tried really hard to make the other be who we each thought he should be. That's no longer twinship; it's control.

We agreed from that moment on that we would no longer compare ourselves to each other and instead free ourselves of the expectations we had of each for the sake of others. We even shook hands and hugged.

The end of Indiana was now in sight, with Minnesota just half a day away.

The trip was a revelation for both of us and we both knew it was something we would not forget. And so it is, with common names and common clothes and common classrooms and constant comparisons to one another, it is no wonder we've spent most of our lives simply trying to figure out who we are. I looked at him sleeping in the passenger seat next to me and wondered if Bobby was ever curious as to why, in the middle of the night, there are times when he knows I'm struggling with something even if he doesn't know what that something is, and so he'll want to call me, just because instinct tells him to?

I wonder if he ever noticed how he looks back at his life and uses pronouns like *we* to refer to himself and *me* to describe the two of us? Does that not give him a glimpse into the way we view ourselves?

But how is our identity shaped? Are we who we are because of our outward and biological appearance (brown hair, blue eyes, 540 T cells per milliliter of blood, and blood type O-negative)? Certainly this was the case with us growing up, where others identified us only by making connections with the other. Our identity, simply put, was *the other twin's brother.*

And certainly this was the case with the research institution, whose very protocol demanded that our twinship be identical; otherwise, there was no room for us there.

Fraternal is a word not directly connected to identity.

But aren't we also something more than our external selves? Aren't we also the sum of our world experiences? Maybe this has been the lesson all along. As children we have no world experiences, so the only thing we have to shape our identity are the features we are born with. And as we grow (alas, away from our shared identity), we take on new experiences, and we take on new loves and new lovers and these experiences move us and shape our identities to the point we are we completely self-realized. Individuated. Whole.

Our world experiences may become what define us, but only after biology has first done its dirty job.

45.

On first arriving in Minnesota, I felt that *here* is blue and green and white. Song in the air: whippoorwill by day, cricket by night.

These were the things that mattered most.

I arrived during January, when the frost performed its wintry dance on my lenses and I stepped foot across the border. The air was cleaner than what I had known. The healthcare, better. The carillon—like a glockenspiel in the center of town—announced my arrival with two tolls of the bell. Any more would have drawn too much attention, so I was grateful for the separation of church and state, and for the telling of time in standards other than military.

The cold was bitter: lungs crackled, skin ossified, and the body's density was the greatest it had ever known. Still, labile, I arrived at this *here* I had read so much about.

And this place welcomed me the way an old house in the woods welcomes the weary traveler. And though the ice-ridden roads shone like black glass even from across the border, there was a measurable warmth in my arrival, in the candle-glow of the moon that January evening.

It is not enough to say that the sky wrapped its landscape around me like a winter blanket. Instead, I must acknowledge the silence of the city sound asleep, unstirred like a perfect cup of cocoa.

I escaped the rat race of Boston (a city of students
makes for transient neighbors). It was a departure that
seemed inevitable: me, with my arms open; the city,
with its fists perpetually clenched. I left it behind
because it was impenetrable—a stone to the knife.
Because if I didn't I would have died. To be living
among the dying meant I had no name—only a Social
Security number, a T-cell count that plummeted like
a trapeze artist at the end of his act, and a long list
of medications that required me to know both the
brand name of each when speaking with others walking a similar path, and the scientific name when speaking with my doctors. (I ask you, what good are any
of those things when the world's most renowned hospitals are all located on the same street, far away on
the other side of town?) I wanted access, to feel the
tributary making its way to the river. The branch
gently folding into the tree.

It's not that I didn't love Boston. It's just that the
place didn't seem to love me, at least not in a mo-
nogamous way, which is what I needed and what any
patient needs of its healer. I said, *Show me*, and the
city said, *Find out for yourself*. So I did. In the country's
oldest subway lines that smelled of pot and piss from
five o'clock in the morning to twelve-thirty at night.
In the parking garages always overstuffed like olives
in a jar, and in the same chat rooms and the same
piano bars where the same men always seemed to
hang out at the exact same time.
    The salve never fully healing the wound.

Boston had its share of seagulls: manic scavengers
bedecked in white robes with name tags and stetho-
scopes, how stone-cold, out of greed, they hovered.
Open-eyed as they scratched and scribbled to take

blood, and always from the same veins. And I observed them, out of the corner of my eye—my peripheral vision always better than my direct—like a child, autistic. Head cocked.

And the carcasses on which those gulls descended searched for love when the world had gone to sleep. Flirted with danger in the infested and haunted waters; they later died with something hanging out of their arms, floating like perfect whales subjecting themselves to the ocean's roughshod slaughter.

It could have been none of these, or it could have been all of them. What I remember is in bits and pieces. Take, for example, the patient who fell asleep while waiting to see his doctor. Or the cars bumper-to-bumper rushing through their routine before the next traffic light blinked again. And God as distant as Boston smiling down on children with clean knickers on Easter.

Yet some things I remember more clearly: my last Christmas there. The midnight hour; the snow in its finest flakes as it blanketed the city like a new coat of paint while everyone outside all at once, as if instructed to do so, stood still. For one tiny moment I could look at the street outside my window not as a place where men bumped into each other like toy soldiers not knowing each other's names, but as a postcard silent in its amber hue, innocent as Currier & Ives and nearly just as quaint. At that moment I chose to celebrate life: the birth of Christ Jesus (who came to cleanse me of my transgressions: those soiled linens on a sick man's bed); the birth of the Christmas Spirit which taught me that once a year I should place others before myself (and to do so any more often would be to deserve whatever kismet should follow); the birth of a new year uprooting itself like a sagging weed and giving way to a fresh, new crop.

Sadly, the soil remained infertile.

And so it became hard to celebrate such life. Hard with a friend shrinking before me like a magic trick gone awry, most undoubtedly his last Christmas, most undoubtedly his last snow, and me not too far behind. Hard when I found myself wearing ice skates I did not know how to use. Hard when my hands were untouched and locked away in a steel box, buried deep beneath the snow and forgotten like a disease for which there is no cure. And hard when I, as a snowman fully clothed and already beginning his melt, fell in love only with trees.

It was my first year without a tree. There was no North Star to guide me. There were no carols on that silent night to otherwise welcome peace to my barren manger.

No gold. No frankincense. No myrrh.

To leave that space was the only foreseeable option.

I came to this place out of purpose. Out of the body's struggle to not become undone. I came to this place with its blue-green-white knowing that there was a me that was here, and a me that was there, and that those twins had no choice but to juxtapose. That is why just after arriving in that once-upon-a-time January I wrote a haiku:

> innocent city
> yet still the moon veils herself
> behind a dark cloud.

That is why just after arriving I wrote that Minneapolis, brittled-boned and wafer-thin, like the broken body of Jesus Christ given up for me, sneaked past my window as if he had reason to lose himself under all that cold ice.

(My wish, it turns out, was simple: snow.)

Seven days had passed since the journey began, each frighteningly emptier than the last. Boston had left me more broken than its fragmented skyline, but here a voice called from beneath the snow. Pulled me along and enchanted me by its lure, reminding me of all I had to lose in this yet to be charted territory.

And hearing it, I stayed.

With the faith of a navigator using only a compass, or the last leaf hanging on to the last tree on the last day of winter, I stayed because something, faint but audible beneath the snow, suggested survival.

46.

A Phase I/II Pilot Study of the Safety of the Adoptive Transfer of Syngeneic Gene-Modified Cytotoxic T Lymphocytes in HIV-Infected Identical Twins. This study is a sequential, open-label, randomized controlled, Phase I/II clinical trial to study the safety of multiple doses of genetically modified T lymphocytes in the setting of patients with HIV infection. . . . This Phase I/II pilot project will evaluate the tolerance, safety, and efficacy of giving HIV-infected twins their uninfected twin's CD8+ T lymphocytes which have been activated to increase their function. . . . In Treatment Period I, patients are randomized in a 3:1 ratio to receive a single IV infusion of unmodified lymphocytes or genetically modified lymphocytes from their respective twins. . . . Gene transfer therapy for HIV infection has not yet been attempted.

Zeta T Protocol
National Institute of Allergies and Infectious Diseases
National Institutes of Health

This experiment was the one that mattered. It was the one that took my brother and me to the National Institutes of Health in Bethesda, Maryland. Our twinship was confirmed identical, and our next step was to meet with the study coordinator.

She introduced herself as Elizabeth, as she stretched out her long, thin arm to welcome us. *Welcome to the NIH. I am your study coordinator, and we'll be spending a good part of today going over the protocol, answering any questions you have, and going over the consent form.* She presented herself with all the professionalism her occupation allowed, as if in all the time she worked with AIDS patients she had never known a single one to die. Bobby and I listened as she told us the details of the study, and we sat somewhat overwhelmed by the strange and unknown universe before us. We met lots of others, each of whom entered the room, welcomed us to the study, and then walked out, like clockwork. There was the principal investigator, a strikingly handsome research physician who I could not look in the eye, and four associate investigators who came in two by two.

We'd like you to meet the director of the NIH and then after that we'll have someone from our legal team come in to provide you with the necessary consent forms, Elizabeth said before leaving us on our own.

There sure are a lot of protocols in this place. Bobby was good at saying my thoughts aloud. *I wonder if everyone has to go through this.*

I'm sure they do, I said. *Otherwise—* I was cut short by the opening of the office door.

Hello, said the next voice, a clean-cut man in a lab coat with a familiar East Coast accent and walnut brown eyes set deep into their sockets. *Welcome to the NIH. We're glad to have you be a part of our study.* He went on to tell us what we could expect in the study, how long it would take before any results would be shared, and something else I did not hear. He stayed for only a few minutes before checking his wristwatch and swiftly leaving.

I then heard something and paused a moment to realize it was my own voice. *Do you know who that was!?* I asked Bobby, a bit incredulous. But before he could muster a guess I said, *That was Anthony Fauci! Who?*

Anthony Fauci. He's the head of the NIH and one of the leading HIV researchers in the world! I said, barely containing myself. *I can't believe we were actually in the same room as Anthony Fauci!*

Bobby put his hand on my knee, squeezed it hard, and said, *See, Tommy. We're in good hands. Everything is going to be okay.*

At that moment peace swept over me like a wave.

Two lawyers then came to provide the consent form, informed us of the risks involved, and answered any questions we had. *We must remind you that gene transfer therapy for HIV infection has not yet been attempted.* We acknowledged the risks for what seemed like the fifth time, and when I picked up a pen to sign the consent, we were told to hold off until the study coordinator returned.

Elizabeth returned shortly thereafter, and I felt my body shudder as she again said the word written in the protocol: *Gene transfer therapy for HIV infection has not yet been attempted.*

It was like being in a movie where you know there will be an end, though you don't know more than that. The study was to divide participants into two groups. Those in the first group held the most promise because they would receive treatment for their HIV infection. The participants in this group would receive genes from their twins with the DNA modified to prevent further infection. Those in the second group were not so lucky because this was a control group. Those in group two would not really receive treatment at all; instead, they would receive the genes of the HIV-negative twin, but the genes would not have any modifications made to them. We were told that once we signed the consent form—which had to be read to us three times by three different people: the nurse, the study coordinator, and the attending physician—we would then be told what group we belonged to.

We found it strange that the study required the NIH to tell people beforehand if they were getting the modified genes or not. *Aren't you afraid that those who find out that they are getting non-modified genes may drop out of the study?* I asked the coordinator.

Her response shocked me. *Well, we expect people to be more mature than that.*

I did not ask it as a question of maturity, but one of life and death. The next day I wrote in my journal:

> Apheresis is a term that refers to the removal of plasma from the blood. The second step of Phase I has Bobby undergoing apheresis. The consent is a decision no one should have to make. A sharp tooth in the mouth of the beast. Dr. X read to me the consent form today. He read quickly and monotonously as if he were thinking out loud and then stopped when he came upon the words "risk of death." He looked at me as if it were the first time I heard

them. He was not moved by my lack of response. I am too concerned about my grouping.

Tomorrow I find out if I am part of the control group or not. The control group does not get modified genes; they just wait on a list for two years for nothing. Actually, the control group gets the donor twin's CD8 cells. Not a treatment; just a placebo. Sort of like a child being led to believe you'll get a triple decker ice cream cone but getting only a glass of water instead and being reminded that water is not a bad thing. All I can do is see what tomorrow brings.

I got the results after I returned home, and the entry two weeks later said it all:

I am unlucky twin #13. Thirteen. Since the time of Christ thirteen has been an unlucky number. This study must be my Judas Iscariot. Surprise. I will receive non-modified genes. I am supposed to be mature, but I am physically ill. I don't think I'll write again for a while. I cannot even put these feelings into words; my words both frighten and fail me. All I want is to go away. No love songs. No promises. No kisses. No candlelight. Only to fade away.

I'm not sure why this felt like school. Perhaps because the feeling was similar to not having my name called when the team captains chose their sides for basketball. Perhaps because I felt the same feeling of failure when it came to things that matter. I wondered if things would be different if I had grown up with plastic lunch boxes, or even small brown paper bags, instead of those damned blue tokens good for one free lunch that no one ate anyway. I wanted to be the one who had a Spiderman lunch box with matching red thermos, but life doesn't always work that way.

Perhaps I would be a different person today, wanting more out of life instead of eating my tuna on white bread, not having time to cut off the crusts that put me here in the first place.

It really was not supposed to happen this way. I was going to be a Ken doll and say things like, *Law school amuses me* through white and perfect teeth. Perhaps it was because I scraped my knees at an early age. Perhaps it was because I ate things like sugar cubes and I did not wear jeans until the age of twenty-five. But Ken never had to develop. He lived his life with blind genitalia, smiling an Ivy League smile, his hands always touching someone else's.

Perhaps if I had been born bare and plastic between my legs like Tupperware in my pants I would never wrinkle, or speak to others in sorry and broken sentences.

The end of my life presented itself before me at that moment. Every moment of growing up with an identical twin, now gone. And though he was hundreds of miles away he felt my pain instantly.

Bobby called to ask me what grouping I was chosen for, and he was not surprised when I told him that I would not be receiving his modified genes. Somehow he had already known because within a week, I received a package in the mail, along with a letter that read:

Gene Substitute Protocol

Dear Recipient,

Congratulations for being selected for the Gene Substitute Protocol. I have heard of your recent notification regarding the NIH's random selection of the twin gene modification protocol, and while it is unfortunate that such twin sets must serve as a control group and, therefore, are not selected to receive gene-modified cells, there is an issue of interest that I feel you may want to explore. Through research, careful planning and non-random selection, you have been chosen to participate in the new Gene Substitute Protocol.

Because of the NIH's recent decision to not pass on to

you modified genes, I felt it necessary to offer you my own personal version of modified genes, which I call the Gene Substitute Protocol, or the Modified Jeans Protocol, not to be confused with the often embarrassing Mortified Jeans Protocol. The Modified Jeans have been thoroughly examined by our own certified laboratory technicians who are highly qualified, and whose conclusions we are very pleased with, as I am confident you will be, as well.

And inside, a pair of blue jeans, modified from their original form. The rear left back pocket was ripped out and sewn to the left front knee, with a rainbow-colored DNA double helix winding its way up the thigh. On the right leg, sewn in blue thread, the word *Bob*, crossed out with red yarn and underneath, inscribed in much deeper blue, *Tom*. On the belt loop rainbow-colored freedom rings to symbolize gay pride. The seat of the jeans contained four patches: a rainbow flag, a pink triangle, and two NBA basketball patches, since he loved to play basketball and chose to believe that after the infusion I would share the basketball gene and it would cause me to take a liking to sports.

That night I wrote in my journal:

For the first time since going to the NIH I shed tears of happiness. It was not unlike the time I drew a dog in kindergarten, when even though you were not around for one of the most meaningful moments of my life, I couldn't have had it without you. I love you, dear brother. I love you.

47.

Gods. They sat on the patios of the restaurants that adorn 17th Street in Dupont Circle, strewn in masses of muscle and cologne. As I scanned the newspaper they were there in the advertisements, sporting buff bodies, even when all they were selling was breakfast cereal. These were the gods among us, idolized by the men in this gay Mecca.

Take the man who sat at the table across from me in an overcrowded café where I had come to hide from the bustling and ordinary world outside. After all, the unnoticeable become more unnoticeable en masse. Yet among the quiet non-gods, humbled by our own bodily failures and misfortunes, a stranger sat. A most holy stranger. Everything about him not only perfect, but immortal. He looked at me briefly while I worshipped him, stricken with a religious awe, as if I were a child in Portugal and he were my vision at Fátima. Like many gods, he did not acknowledge his worshiper and looked away.

There was another god just half a block down. He was standing on the corner with shiny locks of hair and a mastiff by his side. His tresses fell wavy in rivulets, chestnut brown against bronzed skin. He wore no shirt, just a pair of shorts as he stood almost naked, only to remind us that gods have always been known to take on human form. It is a type of mockery, a game played with the rules never fully explained. We cannot be them, but they can be us. But this Samson-like god was unlike the others around him, because on this street most of the gods are bald, parading their domes proudly like sailors returning home. There is something about the lack of hair that calls attention to the gods. Something that baldness demands. A friend of mine once said, *I like a man who doesn't waste his hormones growing hair.* And scientists say that androgen, the male sex hormone, must be present for baldness to develop, thus reinforcing the folk wisdom that baldness and virility go hand in hand. Perhaps these gods are walking vials of androgen, Divine Masculinity among us.

Yet we ask, because we must, exactly where did these gods come from? Did the heavens unfold and drop them like seeds in a garden? Did they happen into this world through some unnamed intervention, an immaculate conception more commonplace than we ever imagined, with holy water their embryonic fluid? Or were they like the saints, born mere mortals and sanctified somewhere along their path? We must know.

My guess is they were born of perfect genes. They ate well-balanced meals three times a day and excelled in physical prowess.

Mortals. Me, despite my attempts to think otherwise, that day in Dupont Circle I felt that I was an ordinary and perishable being. I turned no heads when I walked into a room, and deification was not even within my realm of fantasy. My body was fallible, made of flesh and bone, a vessel of oxygen and carbon dioxide that one day will cease to function. And I knew I was not alone in my mortality.

As I left the café my eye caught a glimpse of a small, flickering light. It was tiny and green and barely noticeable. I followed it for half a block when I realized

it was a firefly. An insect full of wonder and lumi-
nescence. I was hypnotized while it led me to a man
limping as if his feet had betrayed him.

Are you in pain? I asked the man. That's what he
was, after all, a man, and it seemed the humanly, if
not comradely, thing to do. He smiled and said, *I am
okay. I just hurt my foot on the . . . how you call in English?
Ah, yes, the curb.* His accent was Italian. He smiled and
his face was not godly at all. There was a beauty, but
not a balanced beauty. Not like a Michelangelo, more
like a Picasso, where splendor lies asymmetric.

I observed him the way a cartographer observes
a map. My eyes traced the landscape of his face, the
streams of sweat from a humid summer evening. The
hills above his eyebrows that led to the path that
stretched along the nape of his neck. And on his arm,
a valley of scars. Not just one, but dozens, stretching
like tributaries from his armpit to his elbow. They
frightened me, those deep grooves that spread out like
fingers on a hand. *Chemotherapy for my leukemia,* he said,
noticing my stare. *But that was many years ago.*

Time took on a different meaning for me for a moment, and I pictured him as a small child. This scarred
man. *L'uomo sfregiato.*

Do you live here in D.C.? He asked. I told him no, that
I just arrived in town, and that I was taking part in a
study with the National Institutes of Health. *What a
coincidence,* he smiled, *I work there, as a research physician.*

The scars are beautiful, I thought to myself. I was no
longer afraid.

The firefly glowed one last time like a halo behind
the scarred man's head. Suddenly, as if I were losing
my religion, the gods seemed superficial and faded
away.

48.

Being silent I waited for the voice of God. I waited
for the voice of truth and reason to pour down on me
like honey from the sky. Sometimes light, as rain in
Spring. Sometimes ruthless, in buckets. Being silent
I waited for the voice to open my soul and feed me
like a homeless child thirsting for his next drink.
This was the silence I craved.

Instead the silence hid itself behind the *tick tick
tock* of the clock in the corner, and behind the sounds
of squeaky wheels of hospital gurneys and overhead
speakers announcing *Dr. X, paging Dr. X.*

God was hard to find in this place. Earlier the local
chaplain visited me and asked if had any questions of
a spiritual nature that I would like to ask her. *It's okay
to be afraid and to feel alone,* she assured me, not knowing
fear and loneliness were things I've mastered by now.

Why am I here? I asked. *I mean, I'm aware of the study
and that part of it. And I know that I'm not getting an experimental treatment—that I am in the control group and, therefore, getting non-modified cells.* I could tell I was losing
her, so I phrased my question in words I thought she
would understand. *What I mean to say is this: Is this punishment, or is this redemption? I just want to know if I should
be happy that all this is happening to me.*

I took little comfort in her plastic response. *God
is happy that you are asking these questions. It means He's still
important to you.*

At that moment my spiritual life flashed before my eyes. As children growing up Catholic in what is, per capita, the most Catholic state in the country, rituals came to mean nothing to my brother and me. God was empty in each and every single one of them and existed only in the crucifixes that hung above us, reminding us of his death. We needed God to be alive.

When we were baptized in the Baptist Church in late teenage years, I had denied my homosexuality in the blind belief that God made a mistake when He made me this way, and once He saw his mistake He would fix me.

In college, as the secretary of a Pentecostal fellowship, I draped myself in Christianity and shrouded myself with souls as lost as mine. I surrounded myself with the music of John Michael Talbot and Amy Grant, somehow finding God in the rhythms and the sounds meant for others to hear, and not me.

As an adult, first as an Episcopalian, where the incense choked me like harsh words, then at Quaker meetings, where I sat in silence, waiting for God and learning all the time exactly what it means to be patient.

Throughout it all I searched for God. I sought Him in every crack of the city. I looked for His tongue in the ocean's waves, blue and green and wet with nature's fury, all in an attempt to find Him. I swear He was there once, along the shores of Narragansett Bay, where I ran each morning at 5:00, the weight of the wind beating against my chest like a victim seeking refuge. I took Him in like a secret breath. Created an inner sanctum and surrounded myself with candles and holy water. I faced the monastery to the north as if the north would protect me from myself. At that moment my body split in two. One half of me crushed by His weight. The other half, long detached like an unknown twin, kneeling on the beach before dawn has planned her day, facing north with the patience of a dying man.

And I remember God. He was the one who laughed at me from behind the bushes as I braided my hair as a child and made daisy chains in the shade under that tree I called my soul mate. His laughter was soft and danced like a feather in the wind.

I remember Him clearly. Sitting naked in a summer stream, rocks beneath my body, water through my toes, He watched me from a treetop—again His laughter. And He was the one who let me roam. I was the one who walked toward the sun to cast shadows larger than entire civilizations, and His was the laughter that charged forth from the ocean and washed them away. Even in the darkest midnight of my memory, I remember God.

And I remember the conversations I had with Him from late in the evening to the early morning hours. Between us words took root not as a flower that blooms just once and then sheds its petals, its beauty soon lost. Nor as a tree with its branches outstretched reaching vertically, never grasping that for which it spends its life yearning. Instead, words took root like a vine. Wrapped themselves around each other, twisted in the embrace, enraptured, enveloped. Our words became one, a promise, a covenant. Both fruit and blossom, and love showed itself accessible. Widened to the touch, spread itself thin as a veil, and quieted the mind and the unquiet heart. It moved with both the slowness of a day and the speed of a single moment. It spilled like seeds from God's hands, filled with overflow. And I learned, as a child learns, to pick up, to sow, to nurture. Together.

Between us love grew bountiful, beautiful, faithful to us as we tended it. And then, as with all gardens, ours faded with time.

But all this is metaphor. I simply wanted to know how to get back to that place where I once found

God. To recapture that moment in summer camp when I was a child making a God's-eye, the Arts and Crafts camp counselor reassuring me once again, *God is watching you right now. You are unique and wonderful in His eyes, Tommy. And every time you see your God's-eye, you should be reminded that God's eyes are on you.*

Was it possible that with this study I had found God once again in my twin brother? Could it be that after all the roles we had played in each other's lives, I wondered, Bobby would act out the role of Savior? Had I finally reached the end of my life's journey of learning to work with my twin nature?

49.

The doctor made one last round to my room and asked if I had any further questions before my infusion the next day, but I chose not to engage in further conversation with him. That was not why I was here. Instead I made up some excuse that I was tired and needed to rest. I wrote the following in my journal:

> NIH. Infusion tomorrow. Listening to the
> man on the shuttle bus from the hotel
> earlier today about his experience two
> weeks ago, when he was where I am now.
> Corridors smelling of soiled linen. My only
> companions are Charlie, the pool player
> from Iowa, and a styrofoam pitcher of
> water. A TV. Telephone. But nothing left to
> watch and no one left to call. I take comfort
> in believing God's eye is upon me.
>
> I remember rain in springtime falling,
> harvest seeds beginning to spill,
> gardens waking from hibernation, longing to daffodil
> while early morning birds, calling.
>
> There were church bells in the backyard chiming
> on Sunday and puerile songs yearning to be sung,
> sweet morning dew falling gently on my tongue.
> Nursery rhymes, in April, rhyming.
> And northern rivers finally deciding to crest,

a baby's first, peach-skinned complexion.
There was the hope of Easter's resurrection,
little girls in bonnets, golden-tressed.

Lemonade in the summer sun tarting
as children whistled in afternoon shades
and grasshoppers perched atop verdant blades.
The movement under trees was lovers starting.

The carousel at Crescent Park we rode each year
watching sailboats on lakes welcome the sail
beneath sunsets found only in fairy tales.
We shared cotton candy at the state fair.

Swimming in Newport at barren beaches in June,
which stretched itself all the way into September.
Little league baseball games—and I remember
the secrets by porch light, under harvest moon.

I shall miss the chill of autumn's first full-colored splendor,
the evening sky, star-dappled.
A young boy and I biting into apples
with chapped lips that once were tender.

And the walking path from home to school, better
still, the churchyard where we played football
before the Portuguese women wrapped in tattered shawls,
and men mantled in woolen sweaters.

There was danger in climbing the weakened, brittle trees
that dropped their leaves with promises of the sun, fading
over goblins in sneakers, masquerading.
The smell of salt was the ocean's breeze.
I've seen snowflakes falling on the smiling face
of a child throwing snowballs to the sky,

and his mother, not much older than mine, singing lullaby
to the baby she rocked by the fireplace.

And I recognize round men of alabaster smoking corn pipes,
choirs practicing their evensong.
Winter attics full of letters written long
ago. Old photographs. Daguerreotypes.

Snow angels in the field with their wings pearly-white,
images of creches in windows unbroken.
There were candles glowing like gentle words soft-spoken.
The Birth of Christmas Night.

These yearly things, born of distance and time
and body and season.
They tell me they will leave me soon, as if by treason.
As if never truly there, or pantomime.

50.

I found myself standing in a bar the night before being admitted to the treatment facility, trying to make sense of it all. I tried, at that moment, to capture my thoughts:

With my computer, it is easy to refresh. To clean up my mess and start anew with a clean slate I need only press one button. Just one. One button. Virus gone. Press one button and my computer is clean and ready to start anew. Ready to erase the old mistakes and face the new ones along its path.

I do not refresh so easily.

It was this thought that helped me explain what I was thinking as he walked behind me as I stood in the corner of the bar and waited. I did not turn to look. That would have been too vulnerable a thing to do. I waited. I did not turn to look. I did not turn to look vulnerable. Instead I waited. I waited and watched with eyes opening and closing in the back of my head. In the back of my head. My eyes were opening and closing and watching him.

The words then came one by one. One by one in an order I could not comprehend, getting lost in the music and the smoke. I heard the words *I* and *forty seconds* and *I don't know* as they floated from his mouth to the back of my neck and lingered in my inner ear and I nodded. I nodded pretending to make sense of everything in the world at that moment. We talked of Senate confirmations and the dying Popes, life support systems, three centuries of folk and decorative art, terrorists among us. We talked and we tried to make sense of everything in the world at that moment. And one by one his words played themselves in my head like a grammar lesson out of sync with the rest of the conversation. *I arrived just forty seconds ago.*

At that moment the world seemed so solvable.

It was your aura I felt. This is what I later told him when his tongue allowed mine to speak. *It was your aura I felt, breathing its warm breath on my back. It was your aura I felt,* I told him.

His wink: *That was not my aura.*

I do not refresh so easily. I repeated this thought over and over and over again. Refresh.

And I did not turn to look at him. Turn to look vulnerable. Instead I waited as his aura caressed me and breathed its breath on my back. I waited as it pulled me toward him. Pulled me like a beautiful magical thread through the eye of a needle. The pull a magical thread. It moved me out of his range of vision. Moved me to help him see the universe spin before us. I moved. Moved again. Stepped back. Mumbled out of the corner of my mouth, *See anything you like?* Mumbled, all the while feeling the pull.

We were watching the universe unfold before us and I asked if he saw anything he liked. I coughed. Coughed as if to stop my words from leaving my mouth. I coughed and wanted at that moment to tell him that was not me. That was some voice that infected me and now looks like me and speaks like me and acts like me but that was not me. It was my viral twin. Not my thought. Not my words. Not me.

I moved to help him see the universe spin before us. I moved. Moved again. Stepped back, somehow knowing what would happen. As predicted: *What brings you to town?* He muffled through the sounds of the crowd. The sounds of the crowd, the sounds of cigarettes being snuffed out. The sounds of feet shuffling.

The sounds of glasses breaking and always the pulsing bass. The bass pulsing. Always. What brings me to town is what caused the hairs on my neck to straighten. To free themselves of the warmth of his words that floated from his mouth to the back of my neck and lingered in my inner ear. *What brings you to town?* What brings me to town is the treatment for this virus that snaps itself inside me and regenerates like his words repeating themselves. Like his words repeating themselves in my inner ear. Regenerates like his words. My stutter was not accidental: *I'm here for treatment. I'm here. Yes, for medical treatment.*

Words, repeated often enough, can choke a person. Virus scan. Infected. Repair. Refresh.

51.

The lights were out and the hospital room was as black as night. I knew I was not alone; there were endless thoughts of Bobby being there with me, in some strange way, and there were footsteps of the nurses in the hallway. I would tell time by those footsteps. I would tell time instead of allowing myself to drift off to sleep.

This was the first time I had ever slept in a hospital. I was afraid to go to sleep. Something about waking up in a hospital frightened me. I could become more comfortable, I realized, but then I would have to get used to this, and that was something I hoped I would never have to do.

Is this what death would sound like to the twin who has somehow lost his brother along the way? Like a humming silence in the foreground and the sounds of monitors beeping in the background? Perhaps my own death will sound this way. Perhaps after all is said and done, it won't happen like that at all. And instead my body will be an ocean, and all its shared parts—my liver, my kidney, my heart—will drown among the flotsam and jetsam. Perhaps on the bus I take to work some warm, dry morning I'll start to leak from my pores, turn blue, and breathe three times before my descent. Who knows? Perhaps then I will taste bile and think it to be seaweed, and my intestines will split and scatter the morsels of me on the ocean floor to be eaten by whatever lurks there. Perhaps my hair will fall out and I'll roam the world like a cancer patient, shriveled up enough to play the part, while my body—ocean still—emits its spume and waits for the next visitor.

Perhaps there will be no next visitor. Perhaps it won't happen like that at all, and instead entire gospel choirs will line my bedroom wall, and servants will feed me only seedless grapes, since seeds are what caused this in the first place. And perhaps my arms will reach wide enough to embrace the choir in my room, wide enough to embrace entire solar systems. Perhaps my legs will grow even longer, and my feet will turn to stone and I will be firmly rooted like a crag somewhere between Portugal and Scotland. Perhaps my hands will fall silent, as if wading through water, or waiting to be read, and the half-moons in my fingernails will instead disappear and not remind me of the time I have left. Perhaps I'll evaporate, once again, into silent ether and then others will finally be able to tell me apart from my twin.

Perhaps it wouldn't be anything like this at all.

52.

Like an old slide projector, that evening brought snapshots to my mind. It seemed that one minute my brother and I were children running down the steps to the school cafeteria, with hands touching both walls, and the next we were considering the answer to the question, *What do you want to be when you grow up?* It isn't easy letting go of that question.

As a child I believed in Prince Charming and happily-ever-after. There were nights when I would lie awake holding nothing but a candle, shivering as the cold-hot wax melted down my hands. I believed in a handsome Santa Claus, six-foot-two, body hard as stone, eyes tender as clouds. Back then it was easy for me to wish on every fallen star, and even easier to wish on those that were still in the sky, as long as I believed they were falling. When I did, I spent the next day looking for what I had wished for. That was my childhood. I've long since emptied my pockets to the night. I've turned my face from the stars to the city lights. I've spent too many Christmases alone to believe that every evening sound means the landing of tiny reindeer on my roof.

The only real comfort I felt as a child came at those times when I sought solace in the lining of a cardboard box. At first, I pretended it was a layer of protective gauze, and then a roomful of wood and tile, each different in its own way, each design unique, as if to say, *This is what things are made of.* The walls of my youth embraced me not like a steel cage but like a wooden blanket. I imagined that I stripped each piece of wood myself. Sanded and varnished the planks before folding them into themselves and lining them up together. Splintered tongue tucked into hungry groove. These were my walls and no one else's. They were nicked and marred by me, not seeking to be perfect in any way. They simply were, the way a tree is. Merely sliced instead. The wood was lonely pine, the stain a golden hue. Gold. The color of inspiration. At times I roamed the ether world around me with a sense of caution and mistrust. Walking as if with fingertips. I slithered with snake. Leapt with kangaroo. Adapting only as words and artists do.

This, after all, is what childhood is all about, although it came rarely, if ever at all. The night before the first treatment, I found myself letting go of all those visions of my youth. All those snapshots coping with themselves.

They were all a part of me; without me they could never have existed. This was what I told myself to feel wanted again. This was how I reminded myself that all those yesterdays I tucked away were once todays. *This is what you are supposed to do when you are dying,* I once read.

He looks as though he needs to rest, one of the nurses said in a voice so mechanical it sounded unreal. Her name was Victoria, a name much too regal for someone who monitored my vital signs every three hours. She turned out the light as the nurses left, leaving me with only my snapshots.

There was a radio next to my bed with a soft blue light. It reminded me of the plastic beige radio of my youth that caught only two AM stations on its best nights. Its orange light glowed like a flashlight sandwiched between bed sheets; its songs carried me like a magic carpet to the jungle where lions slept. There

were men jumping off bridges in my head. And
cold turbulent waves that opened their hungry arms
before the swallow. Little boys were swimming with
each other unclothed, with bodies smelling of chlo-
rine and almost sulphur. And God as distant as
Boston was smiling down on them. I envisioned myself then having snapshots of that day. I'd look back
and see myself sitting curled up in a corner like a
prisoner in Walpole rocking back and forth, eating
nothing but chalk to survive. I'd see a man with a
city between his legs once gay and alive like Beirut
before the war, before the rapes and pillages, when
the ruins were sturdy and erect and people came from
all over just to see. I'd watch myself, long, thin as a
thread, being sucked through the eye of a needle
and left amorphic and useless in my own quilt.
Perhaps purple mountains in fields of snow. Clouds
like stars on canvas skies, and I, unidentifiable if not
for my eyes.

My brother and I entered the study in April and for sixteen weeks his
genes were replicated for the big transfusion. I decided to stay with the
study, though at the time I was not sure why. Perhaps I felt, after having come so far, there was no turning back. Perhaps I realized that
there was a benefit to it all, even if I was in the control group. Or
perhaps I was more mature than I thought. Nevertheless, the study
had already done its hard job of reuniting us even if I wasn't receiving
modified genes. They said that from that point on my brother was no
longer needed, but that was only them talking, not me. As I saw it, I
would visit this place continuously for the rest of my life for monitor-
ing, and each draw of blood would include a little bit of Bobby.

The thought of infusion drew me closer to Bobby than I had ever
felt. Beginning the next day he would be literally inside me. In my
liver, stomach, brain, heart. I wondered, what would that feel like?
Funny, but it seemed like all my life I had struggled to maintain my
individuality from him, and now, after finally achieving my sense of

self, I would be eternally melded with him. Only this time I welcomed the challenge.

I repeated to myself those thoughts that seemed to follow me throughout those hallways: What if this treatment proved successful, and instead of reminding myself that the official diagnosis is—and will always be—AIDS, I would convince myself that my body is once again brand new? There would be a mourning of sorts, having lived my life betrothed to my beloved only to find my beloved was now undetectable.

There would be a mourning indeed.

I suspect I would have to learn to live again, a form of rehabilitation for the dispossessed.

53.

The day of the infusion I dreamt that morning came and the sun disappeared. It was there for just a moment and then all of a sudden, it simply, without notice, disappeared. The sky did not turn black as night. Instead it was a purplish blue, and there, where the sun would normally be, was a black hole. A small round black hole, like a mole on the skin of the sky.

I turned on the news and found the disappearing sun to be the topic of the day. *Scientists cannot explain it*, one newscaster announced. *This has never happened in the documented history of the world.*

Documented history? I repeated. As if it suddenly hit me that there is more than one type of history—that which is documented, and that which is not.

The disappearance of the sun is only one phenomenon we see today, the newscaster continued. *Equally disturbing is the black hole that rests in its place. It seems to suggest that something—or perhaps nothing—exists behind our known universe.*

Documented history. Undocumented history. Known universe. Unknown universe. The world was becoming larger and larger by the minute.

What was the sun trying to tell us? Was she tired, needing a rest from her daily routine? Or has she found the need, like the rest of us, to be replaced by everything or nothing at all?

I woke up to find the sun did not disappear. It was actually shining through the hole in the window and I was somehow relieved. Maybe it was because I was getting Bobby's genes that day. Maybe it was because I did not die in the hospital overnight. I was not sure. The nurse came in to tell me that the infusion would take place sometime around 1:00, and I could do anything I wanted until then, as long as I did not leave the floor. Hers was the friendliest face I had seen since I'd been there.

At 1:00 two other nurses came in. One had a machine that looked like a little black box. She said that she used it to read the amount of oxygen in my blood. The other had a small pouch containing a cream-colored liquid. *These are the genes*, she said, with eyes dilated. *I bet you're glad to see these.*

In no time they had me ready. One nurse stuck a huge catheter in my arm that wormed its way inside me like a cold finger from an old man's hand. The other carefully observed the black box that connected itself to my finger with a long sinewy clamp. Once the infusion began, the first nurse agitated the bag every fifteen minutes while the other took my temperature and blood pressure, then checked the oxygen levels in my blood. We played this game for the next hour.

> You and i
> we, two, became one
> and the poet asked,
> *when did that happen?*

So this is it, I thought to myself. *Here I lie, lonely as a playground in winter, having my twin brother infused through an IV tube into a vein in my arm.* My body remained stiff, like a violin bow singing a silent requiem. It was official, and ironic. All our lives we had been in competition, unwittingly stripping each other of identity and individuality. We had become the pawns that attack each other long after the other players have left the game. We had lived our lives to be anything but similar, rebelling against ourselves in order to claim our selves. Now, as I received ten billion of his genes, he was literally a living part of me. What was it like to be infused with him? And what does it mean to carry bits of him inside me now, both those I love and those I resent?

Would my brother once again trust me with these priceless pieces of him?

Something inside told me I should be angry with this life. Angry with our parents for not separating us earlier in life when the opportunity presented itself in kindergarten. Angry with God for making access to Him as difficult as trying to stop a train from running its course. And angry with Bobby for taking away my autonomy before it was ever in my grasp, and for destroying the perfect symmetry of our lives, a symmetry which he himself created. A symmetry that left him healthy, and me with an uncertain future.

But all this was futile now because, with him inside me, the past and present of our lives fused together. Being angry with him meant being angry with myself, and I'd no space for anger or tears. I needed every resource I had. Instead I allowed myself to return to a time before AIDS discovered me. A time and place not as lonely as that antiseptic and sterile room, where not even a whisper was heard. But to a place where butterflies filled my veins. Where open wounds gently closed themselves up like praying hands.

A place that brought me back to our beginning.

> The Lord said to Rebekah, *Two nations are in your womb, and two peoples from within you will be separated; one people will be stronger over the other, and the older will serve the younger.*
> —Genesis 25:23

This is our story. From the days of Genesis, twins have always been a phenomenon. Caught between the need to belong to each other and the need to be separate, we live our lives never fully in one place. I suppose one could say that we all have that duality, that desire to be alone and with others at the same time. Some may say that on a basic level, people need people, while others may say that there is no greater loneliness than the loneliness you feel with others. Perhaps life is nothing more than an exercise in balancing the two. Perhaps identical twins are placed on this earth as a simple reminder that there is no such thing as an individual identity, since we are all a part of someone else's.

All I know is that as identical twins we begin our lives in perfect symmetry, and as we go on living, the equation of our lives becomes much more complicated and unbalanced and asymmetrical. And though we struggle to be separate from each other, we are forever inseparable.

I once read that the Japanese have a word for it: *wabi*. Wabi is poverty. Imbalance. Asymmetry. Imperfection. Wabi is the aesthetic quality given to a particular flaw. It is the beauty one finds in the chipped plate or in the cracked teacup. Wabi tells us that each fallacy is beautiful, even divine, because the small yet significant moment when the perfect became imperfect—that brief, special moment—is separated from all other moments in time. Wabi is the fertilized egg the moment it decides to split itself in two. It is the twin god that suddenly becomes mortal for his brother.

Wabi is our self, divided.

Epilogue

My brother's blood was separated into microscopic components before being infused into my hungry veins. In the ten months following I received billions of Bobby's unmodified genes, and ultimately, those who received their twins' modified genes did not show anything more remarkable than those of us in the placebo group.

We joke that the modified jeans he made me were more remarkable than the placebos, but deep down there is a strange comfort in knowing that doing nothing is a noteworthy accomplishment.

For those ten months Bobby and I advanced science in several ways, and in doing so became the best of friends. *Like basketball yet?* He quips. *Cuz that's deep in my genes.* I take comfort in those little moments, something about carrying a bit of him inside me makes me want to nurture that bit. We both feel responsible for the other, and that is a side effect of the study that appears nowhere in the protocol.

We have learned it is possible to contribute even as placebos, and we have shown researchers that gene therapy is a possible treatment option for HIV. But perhaps most enlightening is that even now, over twenty years later, when my blood is drawn, researchers can track the vectors inside my cells; this enables them to identify those genes that initially came from me, and those that initially came from my brother.

In other words, the genes that circulate inside me now—the same genes that will continue to circulate inside me until the day I die—those combined genes that belong to both my brother and me are proof positive that only after being completely merged, are we now no longer identical.

Acknowledgments

This memoir is the result of two young boys, inseparable in their childhood, who desperately and dangerously grew apart from each in order to learn how to live. It is also the product of two grown men, putting aside their newfound differences in order to learn how to love. I am grateful for my twin brother, Bobby, for sharing his life, his differences, and his genetic material with me over the years so that we might navigate this uncertain world together for just a bit longer.

This memoir is also the result of endless rollercoaster rides of experimental trials and protocols over the years. I would be remiss if I did not thank my husband, parents, and siblings for never failing to maintain their faith that we live to tell the story.

Thanks, also, to my MFA writing instructors at Hamline University in St. Paul, Minnesota, who taught me how to hone my creative process and to not be afraid to delve into those matters that have a way of darkening the mind and atrophying the memory.

And thank you to the following publications in which portions of this memoir have previously appeared: *Two Hawks Quarterly*, *Sport Literate*, *Water~Stone Review*, *Talking Stick*, *Gulf Coast*, and *Willow Springs*.

Last but not least, thank you to the entire publishing team at Howling Bird Press, for believing in this memoir and for never losing sight of the forest.

John Medeiros is a poet, memoirist, identical twin, and lawyer. He is the author of *couplets for a shrinking world* and co-editor of *Queer Voices: Poetry, Prose, and Pride*. His work has appeared in numerous anthologies and literary journals, and he is the recipient of two Minnesota State Arts Board grants, *Gulf Coast*'s Nonfiction Award, and the AWP Intro Journals Award. His works have been nominated for a Minnesota Book Award and recognized as a "Notable Essay" in *Best American Essays*. He has an MFA and a JD from Hamline University, and he lives in Minneapolis, Minnesota, with his husband and their menagerie of pets.

About Howling Bird Press

Howling Bird Press is the book imprint of Augsburg University's Master of Fine Arts in Creative Writing program. Students enrolled in the publishing concentration, a two-semester course sequence, run the press while studying the publishing profession and the book trade. The press sponsors an annual nationwide contest, which is judged by the student editors and senior faculty of the Creative Writing program, and publishes the winning manuscript. The author receives a cash prize, book publication, nationwide distribution, and an invitation to read at the MFA program's summer residency in Minneapolis. The contest is open to manuscripts of poetry, fiction, and nonfiction on an alternating basis. This year's title, *Self, Divided* by John Medeiros, is the winner of the 2020 Nonfiction Prize. Our previous books are *Irreversible Things*, by Lisa Van Orman Hadley, winner of the 2019 Fiction Prize; *Simples*, by KateLynn Hibbard, winner of the 2018 Poetry Prize; *Still Life with Horses* by Jean Harper, winner of the 2017 Nonfiction Prize; *The Topless Widow of Herkimer Street* by Jacob M. Appel, winner of the 2016 Fiction Prize; and *At the Border of Wilshire & Nobody* by Marci Vogel, winner of the 2015 Poetry Prize. Howling Bird Press books are distributed by Small Press Distribution; they are available online and in bookstores nationwide.

Howling Bird Press wishes to acknowledge our editors Albert Breton, Makia Jama, Kristine Joseph, Nicholas Lindstrom, and Annastasia Schwab. The press also thanks Augsburg's MFA faculty, mentors, and staff, including MFA Director Stephan Clark, Associate Director Lindsay Starck, and MFA Administrative Assistant Kathleen Matthews. We thank English Department Chair Robert J. Cowgill and Augsburg President Paul Pribbenow. Special thanks to the supporters of the Howling Bird Press Publishing Fund, who—through Augsburg's Give to the Max campaign—provided generous support for this year's project, including Jacob M. Appel, James Cihlar and William Reichard, Cass Dalglish, David de Young, Katherine Fagen, James Lenfestey, Diana Lopez Jones, Paul Pribbenow, Hilda Raz, Julie Sanford, Carolyn Schueller, Lisa Van Orman Hadley, Cole W. Williams, and many more.